Trams in Britain and Ireland

Capital Transport

First Published 2002

ISBN 185414 258 5

Published by Capital Transport Publishing
38 Long Elmes, Harrow Weald, Middlesex

Printed by CS Graphics, Singapore

Photographic credits

Mike Ballinger	102, 107, 108, 109, 111
Beattie Media	31
Capital Transport	4, 60, 136
Peter Fox	121, 142
GMPTE	100
James Harkins	96, 97 top
David Holt	89, 90
Paul Jackson	133, 135, 137
John Laker	5, 6, 95, 97 bottom
Andrew Macfarlane	91
Nottingham Express Transit	116
Brian Patten	59
Martin Petch	129
Mike Russell	8, 9, 66, 92, 93, 110, 113, 115, 130
Colin Stannard	1, 86
Michael Steward	62, 63, 64
SYSL	141, 143
Transport *for* London	44, 83, 85

The front cover photograph is by Mike Russell

INTRODUCTION

The first generation of electric tramways in Britain was largely built, or converted from existing horse tramways, during the first decade of the 20th century. In many cases the local authority tramways were profitable for a time but any profits were often used to subsidise the rates and no funds were set aside for renewals or improvements. As the century progressed the motor vehicle was becoming much more reliable. Buses began to offer greater comfort and real competition to the trams. New housing estates were growing up well beyond the tram termini and it was much cheaper to provide a bus service than to extend the tram tracks. Traffic congestion was increasing and the trams were often blamed for causing obstruction. The fact that passengers in most cases had to board and alight in the middle of the road was obviously a hazard. The introduction of trolleybuses which could use the electrical infrastructure of the tramways, but did not require rails and could pick up and set down passengers at the pavement, was seen as a considerable advantage.

In 1931 a Royal Commission on Transport recommended that no new tramways should be built and those existing should gradually be phased out. The writing was on the wall for the tram; a few systems had already been abandoned or converted to trolleybus operation but the process accelerated. By the time of the outbreak of the Second World War in 1939 trams were on the decline, although even in 1945 there were still around 6,000 trams in service in Great Britain. Some cities made valiant attempts to upgrade their system by moving tracks onto roadside or centre of carriageway reservation, segregating services from the all-conquering motor car where possible, and buying modern tramcar fleets to compete with diesel buses. However, one by one, these tramways fell, with Leeds in 1959, Sheffield in 1960 and Glasgow in 1962 being the last of the city tramways, and even Blackpool reducing to just its long inter-urban coastal line by 1964. That the one remaining line of Blackpool's tramway should have hung on through the lean years as mainland Britain's sole commercial tramway was nothing short of a miracle.

First generation trams in Glasgow towards the end of their career.

A street scene in Amsterdam.

Beyond British shores, the rise in importance of the private motor car also challenged the existence of many tramways and light railways, and many systems went the same way as those in Britain. However, there were exceptions which lasted long enough to visualise an alternative future. Where public transport was still required to move large numbers of people, there was a trend towards the construction of metro lines. In some cities it was not always practical to construct overnight the type of underground railway network that had developed much earlier, but over a long period of time in London, Paris or Berlin. One solution was to develop a full metro system by putting tramways underground in stages, leaving the introduction of metro rolling stock until lines were completed. If trains could travel underneath the streets, then so could trams. Ramps were constructed to take trams underground to avoid the congested heart of the city. After all, the concept was not new – London had already achieved this with the Kingsway tram subway, with trams descending below the streets to reach special sub-surface platforms in the tunnel at Holborn and Aldwych.

So, all over Germany, and in Belgium, and Vienna, the pre-metro process took off in a big way. Many tram systems survived only because it was possible to clear trams from city streets so that the motor car could continue unimpeded. In some cities, pre-metro involved sharing stations with trains, and even using the same tracks, with dual height platforms being provided where necessary. The tram survived because it could continue to be the rail mass-mover in the suburbs, often on its own reservation, whilst it could still penetrate the heart of the city, albeit in tunnel. Outside Britain, the tram could assume the role of a train more easily because the norm had been for tramcars to be single rather than double deck, with extra capacity being possible by using trailer operation.

During the 1960s, and more so after 1973 when an end to cheap oil caused substantial rises in fuel prices, a slow realisation that improved public transport might not be a bad idea began to show through. Congested cities like Amsterdam were beginning a tramway replacement programme when a radical reversion and modernisation experiment using long reserved-track sections to bring the benefit of speed proved that trams could attract patronage back to public transport if the advantage was sufficient. During the 1970s and 80s the light rail revival in Europe and, more surprisingly the USA, took off. Many surviving tram systems were upgraded to achieve speedy uninterrupted journey times which could offer an effective alternative to the motor car. Coupled with the tramway improvements came road calming and traffic management, effectively fettering the freedom of the motor car even more than its self-inflicted traffic congestion. Whilst the bus could be given some special right of way to give it the advantage of speed, the bus failed to gain the public perception of modernity and efficiency that the modern tram had captured.

As usual, Britain was slow to seize the initiative. The benefits of metro were clear, but costs increasingly became a prohibitive constraint. Light metro with greater versatility and lower costs than conventional metro eventually took off in Newcastle, with the first part of that system opening in 1981.

The late 1980s saw a plethora of light rail plans which may have gained public funding and could now have been up and running. However, this is not mainland Europe, and the decade in question was famous here for its right-of-centre politics and severe aversion to 'public' anything, especially transport and spending. If any of the new light railway proposals were to see the light of day, a radical rethink on funding was essential. The alternative method of funding to emerge was the *DBOM* concept – *design, build, operate and maintain*, with private capital mixing with a small public grant to finance design and construction, but with operations remaining with the private sector who would then profit from the revenue earned. Any thoughts of an operating subsidy were right out of the question. To obtain any public finance, each scheme then had to work up a *Section 56* grant application to be approved by the Secretary of State for Transport, demonstrating the benefits of the scheme, not only to potential users, but also the benefits to non-users. Approved schemes would then have to join the queue to await the release of public funds to be drip fed by HMG's treasury.

There had long been a desire to build an underground line to link up Manchester's main railway line termini, but the function of this idea was eventually satisfied by an extremely bold idea. Existing heavy rail trains over lines to Altrincham and Bury, were replaced by modern single deck light rail vehicles. Light rail engineering was used to make adjustments to both rail lines, but mainly to extend the lines so that they were linked across central Manchester using a new street tramway. Another street tramway was constructed to link Piccadilly Station into the system. The result saw the introduction of the modern tramway concept to Britain, and the second generation of tramways in this country was therefore born in April 1992.

In order to build a light rail system in Britain, aside from the question of raising finance, the initial requirement was to secure an Act of Parliament. Powers are now slightly easier to obtain by way of a Transport & Works Order. Land may have to be purchased if segregated running is desired; easements will be needed if these are within existing rail corridors. Local authority planning permission will be essential before infrastructure can be erected, and highway authority agreement will certainly need to be sought for street running.

Light rail is becoming recognised in Britain as a smart, clean and pleasant alternative to other road-based transport and one that can attract people away from their cars for at least some of their journeys into or out of busy areas. In addition to the running or planned systems included in this book, other towns and cities giving serious consideration to tramways include Liverpool, Maidstone and Newcastle.

Blackpool 'Coronation' car 660.

BLACKPOOL

Britain's first and only surviving traditional tramway probably needs very little introduction. Since 1885 electric trams have run on Blackpool's promenade and today the system, operated by Blackpool Transport Services Ltd – a municipally-owned company – extends for 18.4km along the coast of Lancashire from Starr Gate in the south to Fleetwood in the north. This is worked by a fleet of 62 motor trams and seven trailers, which work semi-permanently coupled to their matching motors. The bulk of the fleet dates from the 1930s. Single-deckers from this period are five open 'boat' cars, three much-rebuilt English Electric railcoaches of 1935 and thirteen Brush-built railcoaches of 1937. Seven other English Electric trams work with a matching number of trailers which date from 1960. There are still 24 pre-war double-deckers, known as 'Balloons', in the fleet, of which two have recently been substantially rebuilt with modern steel-framed front ends and one was rebuilt to its original open-top condition in 1985. Post-war single-deckers are eight 'Centenary' cars built by East Lancashire Coachbuilders in the mid-1980s, using many of the parts used by that firm to build motor buses. These are operated as one-person cars. There are also two double-deckers of the 'Jubilee' class built in 1979 and 1982 from parts of earlier cars and also using many components used for bus bodies; these are also intended for one-person operation.

Apart from these service trams, there is also a heritage fleet of eight trams, one of which is a replica. Some of these see fairly regular operation. There are three illuminated cars, one of which has just entered service, and these appear during the autumn illuminations. The fleet is completed by six works cars

The depot is at Rigby Road, just off the promenade at Manchester Square. Most of the system is on reserved track and conflict with motor traffic arises only on a short stretch in central Blackpool. From Anchorsholme northwards the tramway lies outside Blackpool and thus Lancashire County Council is also involved in its maintenance and future.

Top **Balloon 700 and Sheffield 513 (on loan from Crich tramway museum) behind at Tower heading south in July 2001.**

Above **Balloon 701 crossing at Broadwater (to Blackpool).**

Left **Heavily-rebuilt Balloon 709 near Rossall Beach.**

THE NEED FOR RENEWAL

Successive managers and their staff have performed miracles of ingenuity in devising means of keeping Blackpool's fleet of veterans on the road and of executing a great deal of rebuilding in the tramway's own workshops. But, no matter how much effort is put into such a task, there must come a time when it is no longer reasonable to expect such a fleet to cope with the demands of modern traffic conditions, and it seems that this time has now been reached. Average speed is low and the trams do not comply with the requirements of the Disability Discrimination Act – although they are rather more accessible than were most traditional trams. Most of the track and overhead are worn out, although much of the feeder system was renewed a few years ago. Holiday patterns have changed and there has also been a great deal of residential development in inshore areas, well away from the line of the tramway. As a result of all these factors, the tramway operates at a loss, although it still handles large crowds and is popular with residents and visitors alike.

In 2000 Blackpool Borough and Lancashire County Councils commissioned a study from consultants Steer Davies to consider options for upgrading and developing the tramway. Some initial work was undertaken by TAS Partnership of Preston. As part of the present government's transport strategy, money can be made available for light rail projects and the two authorities hope that it will be possible for some of this to come the way of the existing Blackpool line. The plan was submitted to the government in July 2001 and a decision is expected to be announced before the end of the year.

THE WAY AHEAD

The plan envisages development which would take place in three discrete phases. The first would see a complete upgrading of the existing line, with most of the track being replaced and much of the overhead line would be modernised. Stops would be provided with low 30m long platforms and low-floor trams would be introduced on the basic service. Together with priority at road junctions, their increased capability would see a marked increase in speed and a reduction in journey time on the through service from 63 to 45 minutes. As it would be impossible to run at high speed along the promenade – and as no one wishes to whizz down the Golden Mile anyway – the higher average speed would be attained through superior acceleration, traffic management and higher speeds on the line north of Bispham.

This part of the report is illustrated with a photograph of one of the modern Strasbourg Eurotrams, but it is unlikely that these will still be on offer if and when modernisation begins and some other design would have to be used. To handle the peak holiday traffic, some of the existing fleet could be modernised or compatible second-hand trams acquired from Europe. It is envisaged that some kind of heritage service would continue to be offered along the promenade in summer and during the autumn illuminations. The cost of this part of the plan would be around £73 million at present-day prices. As no legislation would be needed, work could begin as soon as funding was assured, possibly after the holiday season of 2002. It is not clear if it is envisaged that the existing depot could accommodate the new fleet or if a new one would have to be built.

The second phase would see the building of a tram line to Blackpool North, the town's main railway station for long-distance traffic and since 1963 deprived of a link to the trams. This line would run on street along Dickson Road from Gynn Square and would continue down Talbot Road to rejoin the main line at

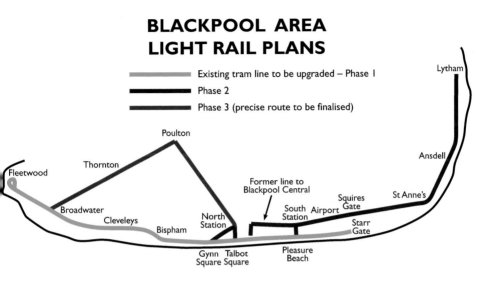

BLACKPOOL AREA LIGHT RAIL PLANS

Existing tram line to be upgraded – Phase I

Phase 2

Phase 3 (precise route to be finalised)

Lytham

Poulton

Ansdell

Thornton

Fleetwood

Former line to
Blackpool Central

Squires
Gate

St Anne's

Broadwater

South Airport
Station

Cleveleys

North
Station

Starr
Gate

Bispham

Gynn Talbot
Square Square

Pleasure
Beach

Talbot Square. This link could reduce congestion in the town centre, as well as creating new travel opportunities. A link is also proposed through Saint Anne's to Lytham town centre. This may use the trackbed of the present line into Blackpool South, which carries mainly local traffic. It would also be able to serve the airport. A short branch could link this new line to the promenade line at Pleasure Beach via Burlington Road. It would also be possible to extend the line inwards to the centre of Blackpool using the trackbed of the former railway line to Blackpool Central, closed in 1964. The estimated cost of the second phase is £74m.

The most ambitious part of the plan is the third phase, which would see the building of a new line, on existing railway formation, from North Station through Poulton and Thornton, rejoining the existing line at Broadwater. Population density in this corridor is already high and several new developments are either under construction or planned, at Thornton and Burn Naze. Cost is estimated at £84m and the exact form of this line would depend on the size and nature of housing developments.

Both the second and third phases would require legislation under the Transport and Works Act and it is therefore not possible to give a realistic time for implementation at present. It is clear that something has to be done soon if the tramway is not to collapse into oblivion. Doing nothing is not an option. It is also clear that the Blackpool tramway as it has been known for the last half-century is unlikely to survive for much longer and for those who wish to see it in its present condition, an early visit is recommended.

This computer generated image showing a tram in south Bristol was produced for the earlier Avon CC 'Westway' proposal.

BRISTOL

Horse trams started running in Bristol in 1875 and eventually comprised 10 routes. Electric trams started in 1895 and the system had 17 routes at its peak. There were 237 cars, the latest being built in 1920 although to the original design. The trams remained open top to the end. Due to the operation of the Tramways Act, which allowed tramways to be taken over by the local council at regular periods, there was a disincentive to invest. Bristol City Council did not use its powers initially. Abandonment began in 1938 but this was stopped on the outbreak of war. Operation finally ceased in 1941 when a bomb destroyed the system's power supply.

In 1979 Richard Cotterel (then a Euro MP) proposed an Avon Metro on the lines of the Tyne & Wear Metro, but more adventurous as it would have required joint running over main line tracks. The proposal suggested Lawrence Hill as the main interchange and comprised a central underground section running east/west and the use of parts of the BR track with lines to Yate, Bath, Weston-super-Mare, Portishead, Severn Beach & the Henbury loop. This idea was never adopted largely due to cost, then estimated at some £400m, and also Avon County Council was at that time committed to road building as the solution to traffic problems.

The project reappeared again in 1986 in the guise of 'Advanced Transport for Avon' (ATA). This time it was planned as a surface system with an initial line to run from Portishead through the city centre and on to Yate. Initially it was intended to be financed by the capture of developer contributions, i.e. from the increase in property values brought about by the introduction of the light rail line. Richard Cotterel announced that it would be 'a free gift to the people of Bristol', a phrase which was to haunt the project for many years. Problems arose right from the beginning. The Port of Bristol Authority was concerned about restrictions on the possible reuse of the Portishead line for freight operations to Portbury. Since the original proposals the Midland line to Yate had been converted into a cycle track so that the proposals to use it for light rail met with opposition from cyclists' organisations. Further opposition came on the political front due to mistrust of the motives and finances of a private company as well as technical concerns.

Despite this a Bill was deposited for the construction of the Portishead to Wapping Wharf section. Although Avon CC did not oppose the Bill, and in 1988 took responsibility for consultation on the project, delays were caused in the parliamentary process due to opposition from a Bristol MP and the defeat of a carry-over motion from one session to the next. The Bill did however finally receive Royal Assent as the Avon Light Rail Transit Act 1989. By this time due to delays and the downturn in the economy any hope of developer contributions

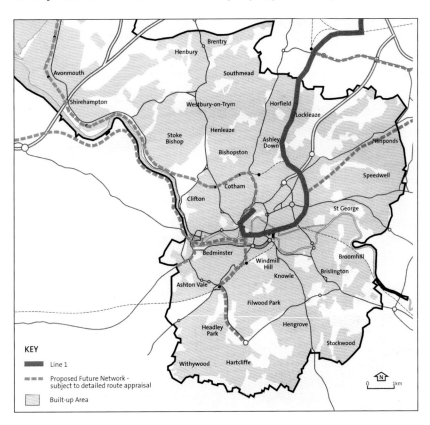

KEY

Line 1

Proposed Future Network -
subject to detailed route appraisal

Built-up Area

had vanished and it was realised that the more normal route of applying for a Section 56 grant would have to be used. Government policy was then that to qualify, a system was needed and not just a single line, so it was decided that work on the Portishead line could not proceed until powers were available for the rest of the system. Studies started into a line to the new town of Bradley Stoke (then in the early stages of construction).

The next Bill to be submitted was for the City Centre section. Opposition from the City Council, who were concerned about the financial implications if ATA went bankrupt, caused delays in the Bill being submitted. It was finally deposited as the Avon LRT (Bristol City Centre) Bill in November 1989. At the same time a second Bill, the Avon Light Rail (No 2) Bill was also deposited to enable the construction of the Eastern lines which were to follow a common alignment to Lawrence Hill then split into two railway alignments to Bradley Stoke in the north and Yate in the north east. This latter bill was subsequently withdrawn to allow ATA to consider further aspects of the alignments, particularly concerning the Yate line. Opposition to the use of the Midland railway line caused a study into alternatives to be commissioned. While this came down on the side of the original proposals, this introduced more delay and cost. Also during this period there were suggestions that the route through the centre, rather than being the double track horseshoe as proposed, would be better as a single track circle round the central area. The outcome of this was that in April 1991 a draft Project brief for a ring rail study was agreed by ATA, Avon County Council and Bristol City Council. As a consequence, the House of Lords Committee did not consider it appropriate to progress the City Centre Bill further until the output of the study was known, and the Bill was rejected. Although the study eventually came to the conclusion that the 'horseshoe' was the best option (with the addition of a spur to Bristol Bridge) financial problems meant that the Bill was never resubmitted.

By this time although Avon CC was assisting ATA, as were First Badgerline (the local bus company) and a report indicated that the best results would come from a mixture of light rail and road pricing, progress was slow due to the financial problems of the company. Despite a report from 'Sustrans', the builders of the cycle way, showing that light rail and the cycle path on the old Midland railway line could coexist, a follow-up study into how to overcome some outstanding problems was never commissioned. There were also problems on the Bradley Stoke route especially in the location of a Park-and-Ride site, the original intention being for one at the end of the line in Bradley Stoke close to the A38. There was considerable opposition to this and the feeling was that it would generate more traffic in Bradley Stoke itself and therefore should be located on the other side of the A38. When revised plans, with the site moved to the west of the A38, went to consultation the feeling reversed. Possibly a growing population meant new people were involved, and the site was now wanted back on the east of the A38.

Despite its partnership with ATA, Badgerline Rapid Transit raised the idea of using GLT (guided light transit) on a route from Hartcliffe to Henbury. The GLT is an articulated bus which can be guided by a single rail and can operate from an overhead supply when guided or from a diesel engine when not guided. Initially this was proposed as complementing the light rail scheme but with the announcement of a route to Bradley Stoke it soon appeared as a competitor and Badgerline and ATA eventually parted company. The GLT was brought over from Belgium on a couple of occasions but no progress was made with the idea.

The financial situation with ATA was getting worse and its desperate attempts to raise money to continue involved being caught out by unsavoury companies and undesirable publicity, and it was eventually wound up. The demise was probably hastened by the announcement from Badgerline of the 'Avon Gorge Expressway' which was a proposal for a kerb guided busway (KGB or O-Bahn) on the Portishead line. This was to be a tidal flow system (into Bristol in the morning and out in the evening with the rest available for freight trains from the Port of Bristol). The cost was initially estimated between £5m and £10m, to be self funded, but once more detailed studies were carried out this cost rose and the idea was eventually abandoned. It did however sputter into life whenever any progress seemed to be made on the light rail proposals.

With the demise of ATA, Avon CC decided to press on on its own although it declined to bid for the assets of the company when it was wound up in 1992. It decided to concentrate on a first line comprising a route from Bradley Stoke connected through the centre to a South Bristol loop. The route to Bradley Stoke being largely settled (apart from the P+R) it concentrated on South Bristol and a route was decided on as the result of studies commissioned. The line was to run from Temple Meads northwards following the line to Bradley Stoke for a short distance before turning eastwards and then south via the Callington Road link to Hengrove, Whitchurch, Hartcliffe and then northwards through to Bedminster possibly partly following the rail alignment and then on to Wapping Wharf to join the line from Portishead. This, with some alternatives, was put out to public consultation, under the title 'Westway', which produced in general a positive response although there were a number of trouble spots where residents were concerned about the effects on their property. A further proposal for the Bradley Stoke P+R was produced which moved it back to the east of the A38. The original site was no longer suitable due to continuing development so it was proposed to use a location adjacent to the A38. Unfortunately this meant the demolition of a recently constructed hotel, which created considerable opposition, and the proposal was dropped.

By this time local government reorganisation meant the end of Avon CC and its transport powers were split between four 'new' councils. The proposed LRT line came under Bristol City Council and South Gloucestershire Council who decided, in the light of the financial tightness of the Government and the difficulties in getting Government money experienced by other cities, that they would concentrate on a route best able to raise private finance. To this end it was decided that only the northern end of the Avon proposals should be cosidered (Bradley Stoke to City Centre). Expressions of interest were invited and out of the response three consortia were short listed (2 light rail, 1 guided bus). The winning consortium (Citylink – comprising Pell Frischmann, Norwest Holst and AEA Technology in association with Railtrack PLC and First Group and supported by Sherwood & Co and Sumitomo Bank) proposed a light rail system comprising joint running with local trains on the Temple Meads to Filton section which would be restored to a four-track layout. Since their appointment studies have proceeded to finalise the business case.

It was indicated that 80% of the total cost (£100m) could be raised privately. The final report led to an agreement being signed by the consortium and the two councils with a small rapid transit team being established by the two councils to carry the project forward.

It was decided that the original horseshoe through the city was too expensive and an alternative, more southerly route was chosen going either past St Mary Redcliff or via Baldwin Street to reach the city centre before turning northwards towards Broadmead, the shopping centre. These alternatives together with proposals for the northern P+R site then went to public consultation.

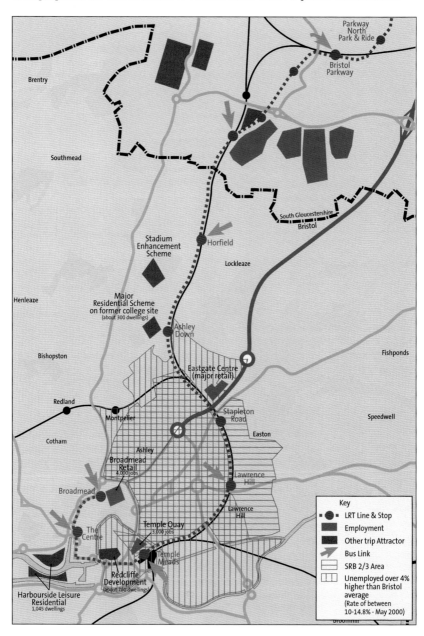

There were three alternatives for the P+R site which occupied three quadrants of the A38/M5 junction: North-West; North-East and South-West. The results of that consultation showed a preference for the NW proposal which used land already in use as a Council depot. This means that the line will have to cross not only the A38 but also get under the M5.

The more southerly route for the city centre was chosen. This has the advantage that although travel time to Broadmead would be slightly longer the route avoided the disruption that would be caused to the heart of the shopping area. Ironically since the decision, plans for Broadmead, if they come to fruition, would mean the redevelopment of a large part of the area anyway.

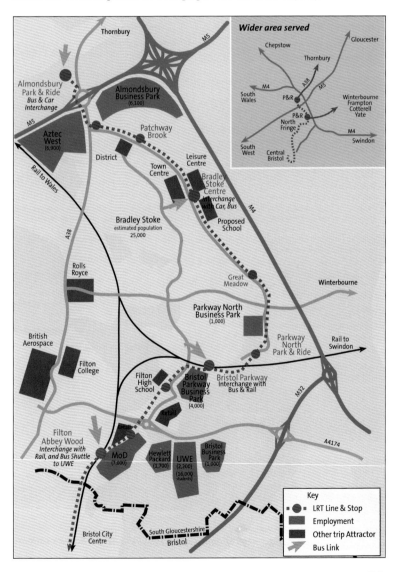

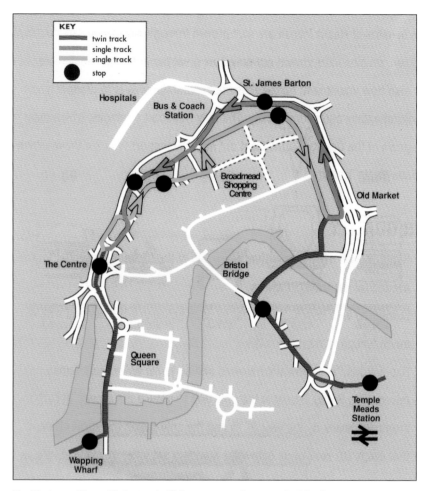

KEY
▬▬ twin track
▬▬ single track
▬▬ single track
● stop

Hospitals

St. James Barton

Bus & Coach
Station

Broadmead
Shopping
Centre

Old Market

The Centre

Bristol
Bridge

Queen
Square

Temple
Meads
Station

Wapping
Wharf

The Westway will provide fast and efficient access to key areas in Bristol.

Work continued in the background both on the route planning and developing the business case but there was little progress to be seen by the citizens of Bristol who despite all the opposition over the years had indicated, in polls run by the local press and the city council, a high degree of support for the proposals. In 1999 response to Bristol City Council's questionnaire on the Local Transport Plan showed that 85.4% believed that light rail would be effective/very effective and received 89.1% support while in a similar study by the Citizens Panel the figures were 85.6 & 90.4 respectively. A survey of business managers indicated 80% support. In 2000 a further poll conducted by the City Council showed that the proposed tram system was top of the City's wish list. With 32% of the vote it received over twice the number of votes than the second item – a new arena, with P+R, a sports stadium and new swimming pool in 3rd, 4th and 5th places.

In 2000 with the change of heart by the Government with regard to light rail, hopes were high that at last some real progress would occur. The local transport plan included the reinstatement of lines to serve South Bristol, Yate via Emersons Green, Severn Beach and also the line between Bristol and Portishead. By this time work was at last being carried out to restore it as a freight line to the Port of Bristol as far as Portbury. Consideration was also given to a plan, known as the 'S' route, to revitalise the existing underused rail lines around Bristol.

Some opposition was by then appearing in South Gloucestershire with regard to the siting of the P+R, with some pressure to route the line to the out-of-town shopping centre at Cribbs Causeway. Pressure was also mounting to add extra stops into the line along the railway alignment. Further difficulties were also arising from the tribulations affecting Railtrack, with doubts that it would be able to carry out its part of the project. The railway refranchising process also caused concern with increased aspirations for the rail network, which if they all came to fruition might not leave sufficient capacity on four tracks for all the envisaged rail services let alone trams. As a result the SRA is now involved in several studies to examine capacity issues and how to accommodate forecast demand.

The year 2001 saw the Government accept the economic case for the scheme and give a provisional commitment to fund a substantial proportion of the cost, now estimated to be some £194m. This is dependent on achieving agreement with Railtrack and also with the Highways Agency in resolving the route alignment through Junction 16 of the M5. In line with the revised funding arrangements being developed with the Government, the Councils have annulled the previous relationship with the Citylink consortium.

Bristol City Council has committed some of its own money, from the sale of Bristol Airport some years earlier, to progress the scheme and the current timescale is to start consultation prior to applying for a Transport & Works Act Order in 2002 with Contractor-bid submission in 2003 for construction starting 2006 and operation by 2007.

A Select Committee of South Gloucestershire Council was set up to investigate the light rail proposals. This heard a wide range of evidence mostly in support but with differing views on the terminus. A consultant's report indicated technical difficulties with the at-grade crossing of the Motorway junction and suggested several alternatives including a tunnel. The Committee, in a majority report, recommended the extension of the line to Cribbs Causeway but, with the danger that such a change would require the appraisal process to be repeated with the consequent delay and the danger of losing funding, if this was not possible in the first stage to terminate short preferably at a P+R to the south of the Motorway. With several studies still to report and agreement still to be reached with Bristol City Council by a Government deadline at the end of March 2002 it still was uncertain what would be the final decision.

During the gestation of the main LRT proposals a tram has been running in Bristol. Under the name Bristol Electric Railbus a service operated by a 35-seat flywheel-powered vehicle operated between the Industrial Museum and the SS Great Britain using lines from the earlier docks railway. Negotiations between the City Council and Rail Property Ltd to extend the line over existing tracks have so far not been successful and without this extension it was not viable to continue the service. It is still hoped that it will resume operation if the required agreements can be reached.

DUBLIN

The genesis of the Luas, Dublin's modern tram system, was in 1988 when the government of the day appointed the Dublin Transportation Review Group. This Group included representatives from relevant Government departments, local authorities and Coras Iompair Eireann (CIE), the state transport company. Its remit was to review transportation planning arrangements in the Greater Dublin Area. The Study, known as the Dublin Transportation Initiative (DTI) was conducted in two phases and issued its final report in 1994.

The DTI was an integrated initiative. It dealt with all surface transport (road, rail, bus, cycling and walking) as well as issues such as traffic management and enforcement. It looked at transport, in the context of how it interrelates with other policies in areas such as land use, economic development, urban renewal, employment and the environment. It was also an open initiative in that it placed great stress on genuine and extensive public consultation. It was concerned to ensure that that the views of all sections of society were identified and addressed. In fact the DTI was led, not by transport considerations alone, but by a broader vision for Dublin. The study recommended inter alia, the construction of a three-line, light rail system at a cost of £300m at 1993 prices.

Following the publication of the DTI report the government requested CIE to begin the preliminary design. Semaly, the French light rail design company were contracted to assist CIE in this. Subsequently the national Development Plan and the Operational Programme for Transport both allocated £200m for the provision of a light railway system in Dublin. Due to the shortfall in the allocation it was decided to build the tram system in two phases.

Phase 1   Tallaght, a suburb in the south-west of the city to Dundrum, a large residential area in the south of Dublin via the city centre.

Phase 2   Ballymun, a large local authority area in the north of the city to the city centre and an extension from Dundrum to the industrial estate in Sandyford.

A general public consultation process was initiated at the end of 1995 aimed at informing the public on the concept of light rail systems. Elected members of the Dail (Irish Parliament) and the local authorities were given in-depth briefings on the project at regular intervals.

The public consultation process received a setback in June 1996 when the Transport (Dublin Light Rail) Bill was unexpectedly defeated in the Dail at second stage. It was purely a political upset and the Transport (Dublin Light Rail) Act 1996 was passed in July 1996. The initial defeat of the Bill had the effect of raising doubts among the media and strengthen the car lobby and those opposed to light rail systems in providing a stage for re-opening the debate on other transport systems. Indeed, the former leader of the Government party undertook a strenuous campaign to have the proposed light rail system scrapped. During this period the phasing of the proposed alignments was also questioned, particularly whether the Ballymun route should replace the line to Dundrum in phase one.

Oscar Faber, Transportation Consultants, were engaged to review the route alignments at the request of the EU and they reported that the original alignment should stand. They did recommend that the design of the Ballymun alignment should commence to ensure that the construction of this line would start when phase one was completed.

Following a general election in 1997 the new Government revised the original plan in 1998. The revised plan was as follows:

❖ A surface line from Tallaght to Connolly Station, a major national and suburban rail station in the east of the city.
❖ A line from Sandyford to Ballymun and Dublin Airport (using the old Harcourt Street and Broadstone railway alignments and with an underground section in the city centre)

It was the Government's intention to proceed with the Tallaght–Connolly Station and the Sandyford–Stephen's Green lines in phase one. This planned phase provides a direct link between the two main-line railway stations in the city, Heuston and Connolly. It also links to the DART, Dublin Area Rapid Transit, a high speed electrified rail system, which travels from Malahide, an extreme northern suburb of the city to Greystones, a dormitory town in nearby County Wicklow. It also links to the main national bus station in Store Street.

DUBLIN'S LIGHT RAIL & METRO SYSTEM

The Dublin Transportation Office, which succeeded the DTI, developed wide ranging proposals for public transport in the city. The Dublin light rail network, Luas, gets its name from the Gaelic word for speed and is being developed in two phases.

The first phase covers three routes already approved for construction by the Minister for Public Enterprise, Mary O'Rourke TD, totalling 24km. This approval followed public consultation, the publication of a comprehensive environmental impact statement and a public inquiry on each of the three routes.

Line A will run for 14km from Tallaght to Abbey Street. Line B will run 9km from Sandyford Industrial Estate to Stephen's Green along the old Harcourt Street railway alignment disused since 1959. The 1km Line C will continue from Abbey Street to Connolly Station, linking the mainline station at Heuston and Connolly and Busaras with the State long-distance bus terminal.

Over the past decades the population of Dublin has grown and major suburbs have emerged on the fringes of the city. Tallaght is a major suburb of Dublin developed in the early 1970s by the displacement of a large proportion of the population of the central city area. It currently has a population of approximately 70,000 and has over 450 manufacturing and service industries.

Line A will have 23 stops between Tallaght and Connolly Station as it passes from the Tallaght Town Square, Tallaght Hospital, the industrial centres of Cookstown and Belgard, through the residential area of Kingswood, Bluebell Drimnagh. It then travels through the major city hospital, James's, past the major main line station at Heuston Station and then into the city centre. From the centre at Abbey Street the tram will continue past the national bus station and onto Connolly Station, a major suburban and national rail terminal.

Sandyford Industrial Estate is one of the largest industrial complexes in Dublin. It is home to some of the largest American and European computer software companies that have established European bases.

Line B between Sandyford Industrial Estate and Stephen's Green will have 13 stops. This line, for most of its route, will run on the old Harcourt Street rail alignment, which has been disused since 1959. On its journey to Stephen's Green, one of Dublin's more upmarket shopping centres, it will travel through the mainly middle class areas of Stillorgan, Dundrum, Milltown and Ranelagh. For a short distance after the Milltown stop the line gradually descends to run at grade. At Ranelagh the line will again be elevated until it crosses the Grand Canal on a newly constructed bridge at Charlemont. From here to Stephen's Green it will again travel at grade terminating at the junction of Stephen's Green and Grafton Street.

Stops for the Luas will consist of raised platforms 300mm high and 40m long with a ramp at either end as required. Where they are situated on either side of the track they will be 3m wide and 4m wide between the tracks. The tram service will stop at every stop. In the city centre the stops will be between 240 and 600 metres apart; in the outer suburban areas they will be slightly further apart.

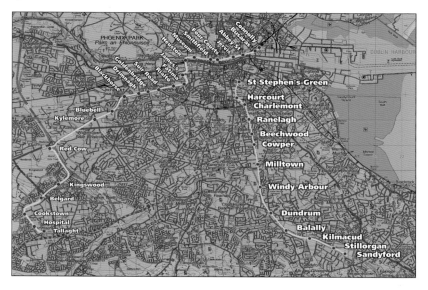

THE TRAMS

Alstom has been chosen as the supplier of the trams that will service the Dublin routes. Twenty-six Citidas 300 trams will run on Line A. These 30metre long vehicles with asynchronous traction, feature partial low floor to facilitate passenger flow. The first tram was delivered in October 2001 with a delivery of two trams per quarter thereafter.

The vital statistics of the rolling stock are as follows:

Width:	2,400 mm
Length (single unit):	30,000mm
Height (pantograph not included):	3,400mm

The main performance characteristics of the tram are:

Maximum speed:	70 km/h
Initial acceleration:	1.2m/s^2
Average deceleration in operation:	1.0m/s^2
Emergency deceleration:	3 m/s^2
Maximum load conditions:	8 passengers $/\text{m}^2$
Slope start:	(minimum acceleration of 0.1m/sec on a 6% gradient with a coefficient of adhesion of 0.15)

TRACK DESIGN AND TRACKBED

The track is to the standard European gauge of 1435 mm. The system will be double track throughout which gives an overall trackbed width of 5.9m on a straight alignment or 6.3m where the trackbed contains axial poles. On curves the distance between the tracks is wider in order to accommodate the swept path of the tram. The rails will be supported by sleepers which in turn will bear on a concrete foundation and or ballast. The minimum horizontal radius of the track will be 25m while the normal maximum gradient will be 6% (in special cases 8%).

Track laying methods will vary depending on location. Normally the rails and sleepers will be mounted on a mass concrete foundation. Close to buildings and in other sensitive locations, anti-vibratory methods such as floating slab track (which incorporates a resilient layer between the track and the foundation) will be used as required.

Where the track runs along a road or a street, a grooved rail will be used and the areas between and beside the rails will be paved-surfaced. The type of paving/surfacing will depend on the character of the surrounding area and the nature of any non-tram traffic which may run over the trackbed. A slight incline will be made in the street surface to define the edge of the tram track in order to provide for an efficient level of service by discouraging other vehicular traffic from encroaching or remaining on the tram route. Only when absolutely necessary will traffic be permitted on to the trackbed, such as in overtaking the tram when stationary or turning manoeuvres.

POWER SUPPLY & SIGNALLING

The trams operate on 750 volts direct current. The National Electricity Supply 10kV alternating current supply will be transformed and rectified to direct current at substations located at intervals along the routes. Eighteen substations will service both lines. Electricity will be supplied to the trams by means of overhead power lines at a height of 6.0m above the ground, supported by poles either along or between the tracks or by cables fixed to building facades. To minimise the visual impact of the overhead line equipment, particularly in the city centre and other areas of civic design, use will be made of anchors to buildings and lamp standards. Power will be supplied to the overhead line via multi-tubular cable ducts which form one edge of the trackbed foundation; on the other side will be a parallel set of ducts carrying communication and signalling cables. The main power supply is underground and is connected to the contact wire at intervals. This will minimise the weight of the contact wires and reduce the amount of overhead wiring in the city centre.

DEPOTS

The depot for line A located at the Red Cow/M50 interchange on the Naas Road. It will cater for the garaging, servicing and maintenance of the trams. All administration and systems control will be situated at this depot. A major rural and Dublin bus interchange together with a park-and-ride facility for 756 cars will also be located there. This depot was completed in August 2001.

The depot for line B is located adjacent to the Sandyford Industrial Estate. Fourteen trams will be stationed here as well as a park and ride for 550 cars.

FUTURE DEVELOPMENTS

The NDP set ambitious targets for the next six years and during that time the government will spend £2.2bn on public transport. The Cabinet Committee on Infrastructure has identified public transport as a strategic priority for a balanced national development and recognises that any delay in the delivery of the transport infrastructure would threaten the entire plan.

The Plan envisages a light rail network far more extensive than the original proposals. There will also be an outer metro ring linking major centres of population in the suburbs. An integrated ticketing system will be introduced.

Phase 2 of the Government's plan groups the remaining lines which are at design stages and will be built between 2003 and 2010. These include Line B1 from Sandyford to Cherrywood which following public consultation is at planning stage, and an extension of Line C from Connolly Station to the Docklands area on the north bank of the Liffey. Further routes under consideration include a north-south line from Ballymun to Dundrum via Whitehall, the city centre, Harold's Cross, Terenure and Rathfarnham, with a possible northern extension from Ballymun to Sillogue. A spur from Whitehall to Kilbarrack via Coolock would provide a northern connection to the DART suburban network. An east-west line will connect Lucan to Docklands via Ballyfermot, Dolphin's Barn and the south inner city, by way of the proposed Macken Street Bridge. Total length of the Luas network could be in excess of 50km.

Trams will run at 5-minute intervals during peak times and at 10 minutes off-peak. Typical journey times from Tallaght to Abbey Street will be 30 min and 43 min to Connolly. Sandyford to Stephen's Green will take 22 minutes.

As part of the National Development Plan the Government announced in mid-2000 that it had approved the development of a metro system for Dublin. This is to be developed on the basis of a Public-Private Partnership, using a design, build, finance, operate and maintain mechanism. Construction of the metro is due to be completed by 2016, together with extensions to the DART suburban rail network. The Light Rail Project Office has been tasked with drawing up the PPP strategy and has commenced the necessary preparatory work. In December 2001 the Minister for Public Enterprise established the Railway Procurement Agency (RPA). Currently the RPA is overseeing the implementation of the three Luas lines which are under construction. The Agency is also involved in the planning and design of the extensions of these lines from Sandyford Industrial Estate southwards to Cherrywood and from Connolly Station eastwards to the Docklands. In response to the government announcement in January 2002 regarding the development of the metro system for Dublin, the Agency has undertaken the first stage of the procurement process.

The Metro network will comprise three routes, operating on fully segregated alignments. Line 1 will run from Shanganagh, near Bray, to Swords, via the city centre and Dublin Airport. This will make use of the outer end of the former Harcourt Street rail alignment and will then take over the section of Luas Line B between Sandyford and Ranelagh, which will be upgraded to full metro standards. From Ranelagh to Broadstone, the line will cross the city centre in tunnel, serving en route an interchange with the DART at Tara Street Station. The orbital metro Line 2 will diverge from the Shanganagh–Swords line in the northern suburbs, and run via Finglas, Blanchardstown and Clondalkin in the north-western and western suburbs to Tallaght. The ring will be completed by Line 3, from Tallaght West to the city centre via Tallaght and Kimmage. This will join line 1 near Ranelagh and share the cross-city tunnel.

EDINBURGH

Edinburgh is unlike other British cities in a number of ways. It is compact and a fairly large proportion of the population lives in the central area. Consequently car ownership is lower than might be expected from the general level of incomes in this area and bus use is still high. Suburban rail transport has not developed to a significant extent and even in the heyday of railways it catered for only a minor proportion of the internal traffic of the city. The main station, Waverley, was built on the site of a former loch and lies below the surface of the surrounding area. The city is built on a bed of consolidated lava from extinct volcanoes and this rock is extremely hard. There has for long been a strong and active movement for the preservation of the architecture of the city and as a result it has suffered much less than others from the attention of both road-builders and developers.

1989 PROPOSALS

The first serious proposal for a modern tram or light rail system was published in June 1989. At that time Lothian Regional Council had overall responsibility for planning and traffic management and also ran the city's bus service. Concerned at the growth of congestion in the central area, the Regional Council established a public transport study in 1987. Consultants and council officials worked together on the report, but there was also extensive consultation with the citizens and with local groups. The area studied extended well beyond the present day boundaries of the city. Various forms of transport were considered, including trolleybuses, light rail and heavy metro.

Artist's impression from the brochure published in 1989.

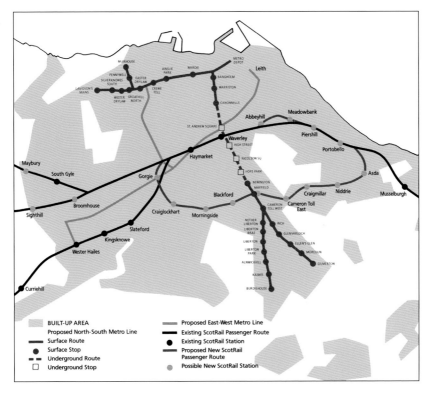

░ BUILT-UP AREA	▬ Proposed East-West Metro Line
— Proposed North-South Metro Line	▬ Existing ScotRail Passenger Route
▬ Surface Route	● Existing ScotRail Station
● Surface Stop	▬ Proposed New ScotRail
▪ ▪ Underground Route	Passenger Route
□ Underground Stop	● Possible New ScotRail Station

The preferred strategy recommended by the working group envisaged a light rail network of two lines. (The term 'light metro' was used to describe these.) The first to be constructed would run from Davidson's Mains and Muirhouse in the north to Gilmerton and Burdiehouse in the south, following in part former tram lines. Total length would have been 17.5km and there would have been 32 stops, including two park and ride sites. Most stops would have been 500m–600m apart. From the northern terminus at Davidson's Mains the line would run on roadside reservation to Crewe Toll, from which it would follow a former railway alignment to Canonmills. On the approach to the city centre, the line would make use of the Scotland Street tunnel which survives from an early railway line in the area, to pass under Waverley station. From there it would run in tunnel, generally at a depth of 30m but on a steeply rising gradient, under the line of Nicholson and Clerk Streets, serving the main campus of the University of Edinburgh, to emerge to the surface again on Minto Street at Salisbury Place. There would be underground stations at Saint Andrew Square/Waverley, High Street, Nicholson Square and Clerk Street and these would have been served by inclined lifts. Interchange with the second line would have been at Saint Andrew Square. From Minto Street the line would continue on surface, with street running, to Cameron Toll, where the branches to the two termini would divide. One of these branches could be extended into Midlothian at a later date. It was estimated that 5% of existing car users would have been attracted to the new line. The capital cost of the north–south line at 1987 prices was £184m.

The plans seemed attractive, but contained a fatal flaw. The underground stations would have to have been located at a great depth and would not have catered for the heavy local traffic flow along the corridor of Nicholson and Clerk Streets. Proposed use of the existing tunnel from Canonmills to Saint Andrew Square meant a distance of 800m without an intermediate station – under an area of dense population – and would have deprived the line of the traffic potential of Leith Walk, a wide street about 500m to the east, where a tram line would have met little opposition.

The second line would run from the large housing estate of Wester Hailes – an area of very low car ownership – through Gorgie to Haymarket, where there would be interchange with main line rail services. It would then traverse the central area, on a line of route to be decided at a later date, and continue via Restalrig to the central area of Leith. The report also recommended the reopening to passenger traffic of the circle railway line which runs around the inner southern suburbs of the city and this would have had interchange with line 1 at Newington. There were also plans for several new stations on existing rail lines.

The publicity material which accompanied the report showed trams vaguely like those operating in Nantes, serving an underground station similar to those of the Tyne and Wear metro. Published dimensions and other illustrations, however, indicated a vehicle more like the trams in Grenoble. The light rail vehicles would have seated 70–80 passengers, with a total capacity of 200 and would have been 30m long by 2.3m wide. There would have been in all 29 cars. Only after 1991 did the Region begin to take accessibility into account, but it was at no time made clear if the cars would have been of high floor design with retractable steps or of low floor pattern.

Having published its plans, the Region then undertook extensive public consultation in the autumn of 1989, with a view to seeking Parliamentary powers in 1990. There was a good rate of response to the consultation but unfortunately the plans unleashed a storm of protest from the residents of Newington, who were and are content to live with the stream of motor traffic which pours through the area daily but who took fright at the thought of trams returning to their streets. When reporting on the plans, the press generally illustrated articles with a photograph of an Edinburgh double-deck tram of the 1930s and the local evening newspaper was strongly against the scheme.

The line was further considered as part of a joint study involving also the Scottish Development Department (an arm of the then Scottish Office) and Edinburgh City Council. An environmental impact study was undertaken in June 1990, with generally favourable conclusions. As a result of these further studies, it was agreed to extend the underground section 2km further south to Cameron Toll and add a short extension at Burdiehouse. The basic cost of the scheme had now risen to £224m and this extra tunnel section added a further £44m. This was equivalent to £15,314,000 per kilometre, a figure which compared badly with the £8.27m (1994 prices) of the South Yorkshire Supertram.

Although the scheme was still expected to show a favourable rate of return and to be able to operate without subsidy, these changes effectively spelled the end of the plans. While some of the blame for this must rest with those who filled the post of Chief Secretary for Scotland in the Major government, the total cost for a fairly short line simply made it unrealistic. In any case, the same government was soon to become much more preoccupied with its plans to dismantle the Region and by 1993 the latter had lost all interest in the scheme, although it was not formally abandoned. The City Council, as successor authority in transport and planning matters, transferred its attention instead to a plan for a busway to serve the western suburbs. This was later refined as CERT – City of Edinburgh Rapid Transit – and was enthusiastically, indeed tenaciously adopted by the Council. This scheme too proved impracticable but was not finally abandoned until 2001, since when the city authorities have looked rather more favourably on light rail.

While both the Strathclyde and the Lothian schemes suffered to some extent from the democratic deficit which then affected Scotland, only in the former case is the failure to be regretted. Had the Lothian scheme gone ahead, it would almost certainly have over-run budget due to the expense of tunnelling through very hard rock and would have provided a system which did not fully meet the needs of the local population. With hindsight, failure was a blessing in disguise.

THE NEW EDINBURGH TRAM COMPANY

In 1996 a company known as the New Edinburgh Tram Company announced plans for a line to run from Haymarket station via Princes Street and Leith Walk to Newhaven, with a branch into Leith Docks. To keep costs down to £40 million, it was intended to use the rail system developed by the LR55 group under the guidance of Professor Lewis Lesley and a lightweight design of tram, the 'Roadliner' of which one example was built and briefly ran trials in Blackpool. In connexion with the project, this vehicle was brought to Edinburgh and displayed in Parliament Square, this being the first tram to grace an Edinburgh street since November 1956. However, public authorities were unenthusiastic and it proved impossible to raise funding for the project.

THE WATERFRONT SCHEME

Since the unsuccessful plans outlined above were discarded, a great deal has changed in transport matters in Edinburgh. Devolution has brought increased prosperity to the Scottish capital and with it has come increasing car use, with accompanying congestion and atmospheric pollution. At the same time, the port of Leith has continued to develop, becoming in the process not only a cargo port but a passenger terminal with regular visits from cruise liners. To cater for these a new ocean terminal has been constructed, which is in fact not only a transport facility and the home of the former royal yacht Britannia but a shopping and entertainment centre. Much of the civil service has also been relocated to Victoria Quay from the city centre. Edinburgh's other and smaller port Granton, lying to the west of Leith, has shared the fate of many other similar installations and experienced decline, this including not only the harbour but also the industrial area immediately behind it. This area includes the site of a former gasworks, dating back to 1824 and the first large scale installation of its kind in Britain.

Public attitudes to light rail have also changed in the interim. Both the Scottish national press and the local newspaper are now strongly supportive of the concept, to the extent that the City Council has been criticised for not acting more quickly!

Bus patronage remains high and has recently increased, largely due to the introduction of 'Greenways' on many main roads, to give buses priority. In Princes Street, private traffic has been banned from using the street eastbound and this has both improved the commercial speed of the buses and the local environment.

To cater for these trends and maintain the quality of life in the central area, the City Council has drawn up a transport strategy based on road user charging. If all goes according to plan, this will be introduced in 2005, when motorists will be charged a sum not exceeding £3 to enter the central area. The proceeds of this charge will be ring-fenced for improvements to public transport. The main investments will be in three schemes:

1   Restoration of passenger services on the former suburban circle rail line.
2   Construction of a limited busway in the western area of the city.
3   Introduction of light rail.

Application is currently being made to the Scottish government for funding under the latter's public transport funding initiative. At present-day prices, the total cost would be in the region of £800 million.

The first line of light rail to be planned takes the form of a loop around the northern part of the city. To bring about the redevelopment of the area around Granton, Edinburgh City Council and Scottish Enterprise Edinburgh and Lothians set up in March 2000 a joint venture known as Waterfront Edinburgh Ltd, which owns much of the land in the area. The remainder is owned by Forth Ports and Lattice Property Holdings. The former has itself shown enthusiasm for light rail in the past. The master plan envisages commercial and light industrial development creating ultimately about 20,000 jobs, 5,000–6,000 dwellings of various kinds, two new schools and associated community and leisure facilities.

To provide access to the area, various alternatives were considered by Waterfront Edinburgh and the choice was narrowed to either a guided bus or a light rail system. It was considered that the former was unlikely to attract additional patronage, while light rail with its modern image and regularity of service would both attract passengers and in itself act as a symbol of the nature of the entire project.

From Granton the line would head southwards on the alignment of a former railway, which is already in the ownership of the City Council. It is at present used as a walkway and a cycle path and there is enough space on the alignment to allow continuation of both of these uses. This part of the line would serve existing areas of housing, Telford College of Further Education and a number of hotels around Craigleith. At Roseburn the line would descend to street level and run eastwards via Haymarket, where there would be interchange with main line trains. It was originally intended that the line should terminate here but further studies showed that it would be more profitable, and much more attractive to passengers, if it were continued eastwards to Princes Street, to a terminus at Saint Andrew Square. However, while such a line would certainly be capable of standing alone, it was then realised that it would form a much more useful facility if it were carried on northwards via Leith Walk to serve the port area and the civil service headquarters. From there it will continue, on an alignment yet to be decided, along the shore of the Firth of Forth, via Newhaven back to Granton.

Total length of the line would be 15.7km and this would require a fleet of 16 trams, each carrying a maximum number of 250 passengers. A six-minute frequency would be provided and a journey time of about 16 minutes from Granton to Princes Street is envisaged.

Publicity material has used illustrations of both Montpellier Citadis trams and Strasbourg Eurotrams. The actual choice of vehicle has yet to be decided, but the trams would be of low floor design. The total capital cost of the light rail scheme is about £192 million at current prices.

The plan conforms with each of the Scottish government's five appraisal criteria, as set out in STAG – Scottish Transport Appraisal Guidance. It is expected to return a surplus on its running costs. It would substantially improve the city environment and contribute to a reduction in road traffic accidents. It would bring increased accessibility to some areas of the city which at present are poorly served and thus increase employment prospects and decrease social exclusion. People with mobility impairments would additionally benefit.

This imaginative scheme has been thoroughly costed and has received support not only from businesses which are interested in the area but also from educational establishments, the local NHS health trust and the National Museums of Scotland. Lothian Buses, the operator of the Council-owned company's buses, is supportive. It is intended that it will be the first of several light rail lines in the city and surrounding area. A rather protracted time scale could, if approval is received in the near future, see the first trams running in 2009.

Artist's impression of light rail in Vincent Street, Glasgow from a leaflet issued by Strathclyde Regional Council in 1994.

GLASGOW

Of all the cities which have at one time or another planned light rail schemes, Glasgow alone has the sad distinction of having planned two separate systems, neither of which has resulted in the construction of a single metre of track.

The first plan dated from 1944. At an exhibition held in the autumn of that year, a model was shown of the tramway of the future. This featured a line running on a central reservation, between semi-detached houses of distinctly pre-war appearance, the overhead being suspended from ornate centre poles which were positively Edwardian! However, there was nothing old-fashioned about the tram, which was a single-decker, clearly derived from the North American PCC car – at that time the most up-to-date type in service – but sporting a bow collector in place of a trolley pole. Following on from this exhibition, the City Engineer, Robert Bruce, published in 1946 a transport plan which envisaged, among other services, a system of routes served by 'electric vehicles'. From various termini on the south side, these would converge into a subway under Queen Street, then branch out to serve Knightswood in the west and Easterhouse in the east.

FARSIGHTED PLANNING IN 1948

Nothing came of this report, but in 1948, as part of the Fifty Year Plan for the development of the city, the General Manager, E R L Fitzpayne, prepared for the transport committee of the Corporation a plan for a light rail network, a plan far ahead of its time and containing many ideas which form the basis of current light rail schemes. The plan proposed the electrification of certain suburban railway lines, separated from the main line network, and the conversion to standard gauge – Glasgow used a track gauge of 1416mm – of certain tram routes, which, with some extensions, would form a unified network with these railway lines. The author stressed the advantages of light rail for these lines, as a means of both spreading construction over a wider area and also reducing staff costs. They would run in subway in the central area and elsewhere would use the median strip of main roads and existing railway formations. Stations would be not less than 900m apart, allowing an average service speed of 40km/hr and it was planned to use a 'skip stop' arrangement, with frequent headways. Platforms would be enclosed, with sliding doors to correspond with the doors on the light rail vehicles. The service would be regulated by three-aspect colour light signals and by other safety devices, possibly including radar. Most of the city could thus be covered by a dense network of railways, either light or heavy.

The lines selected for light rail were:

◇ The line along Great Western Road – already on reserved track for part of its length – extended from Knightswood to Duntocher, with a branch to Kelvindale, using a rail line.
◇ The line along Paisley Road West from Bellahouston Park to Paisley.
◇ A short section at Mount Vernon, to link an existing rail line with line 4.
◇ A line from Castle Street to Dennistoun and an extension to Queenslie via Edinburgh Road.
◇ A line to serve Pollokshaws and Barrhead.

The only new tunnel envisaged was one from Pollokshields to Alexandra Parade via Gorbals and Queen Street, to link lines 2 and 5 with line 4. No freight or main line trains would use the rail routes included in the scheme and no question of inter-running with these would arise. All other tram routes would be replaced by buses or trolleybuses.

The light rail vehicles which would run on the upgraded routes were shown as twin-car units, which could be coupled in pairs, rather similar to Stuttgart's DT4 Stadtbahn cars of the present day. They would, however, use high platforms only. Comfortable bucket-type seats would have accommodated 47 passengers per car and the standing capacity was given as a very modest 30. Two double-width doors would have been fitted per side, their half-moon glass panels being very reminiscent of the 1930s. The seats would have been turned by compressed air at terminal points.

Rather strangely, it was planned to use third rail current collection. The reason given for this decision was that it would ease maintenance in tunnels, but it would also have precluded any possibility of street running.

While the failure to provide for street running would have been a drawback which would have limited the scope of the system, the plan, if implemented, would have given Glasgow a network of rail lines which would have been of great benefit to the travelling public and would have prevented years of decline and perhaps also slowed the trend to private car use which began soon after-wards. As it was, they were much too advanced for contemporary local and national politicians; the former remained paralysed in indecision while the latter were much more interested in favouring the recently-nationalised Scottish Bus Group. A further report in 1951 by a committee headed by Sir Robert Inglis – a committee on which, incredibly, Glasgow Corporation was not represented, airily dismissed Mr Fitzpayne's plans as unfeasible on the grounds of capital cost and nothing came of them. One of Britain's most far-sighted and energetic transport managers was later obliged to preside over the run-down and scrap-ping of what even in 1948 was still an excellent tram system, with considerable potential. Some but not all of the railways included in the Fitzpayne plan were later electrified and the last tram ran on 4th September 1962.

Serious consideration of light rail for Glasgow was not resumed until December 1989, when Strathclyde Regional Council published a consultation report on public transport for the 21st century. This report was based on analysis and evaluation of the responses to surveys which had been undertaken from May 1988 onwards. The report covered all forms of transport within the Region, but its most novel conclusion was that technology had developed to the stage which allowed guided transport to be provided which combined the accessibility of the bus with the speed and comfort of conventional rail services. Developments to date suggested that light rail, rather than guided buses, would best provide this kind of service. The report also looked at possible extensions to the existing underground line, but concluded that these options did not warrant further consideration, mainly because of the limited capacity of the narrow gauge (1219mm) system and the disruption which would be caused during the construction of extensions.

Apart from improvement to certain existing rail lines and reopening of others, the preferred option for development was what was called a partially segregated metro. This would make use of portions of existing rail lines, some disused rail lines, central reservations in main roads and street running in the city centre and at suburban termini. No interrunning with main line services was envisaged and there were clear echoes of the Fitzpayne plan of forty years earlier.

The light rail lines proposed were as follows:

Conversion of the Cathcart Circle railway line, with its branches to Neilston in the west and Kirkhill in the east. This southern metro would be complemented by three new lines on reservation along certain roads. These were a branch from the Kirkhill line to Castlemilk, terminating in a loop, a branch from the Neilston line to Newton Mearns and a loop from Mount Florida on the circle to Pollok. The line would diverge from the existing alignment at Strathbungo Junction and run via the disused St Enoch line to terminate in a loop at St Enoch. The scheme would have the merit of both assisting in the regeneration of two rather run-down areas – Castlemilk and Pollok – and of encouraging commuters from the more affluent suburbs to switch to public transport and so reduce the volume of traffic on roads in the southern part of the city. Congestion in central Glasgow would also be reduced. The capital cost was estimated as £155 million, but £17 million would be saved by not having to replace some existing electric rolling stock of class 303.

By conversion of the Drumgelloch/Airdrie and Springburn lines in the east and the Milngavie and Dalmuir via Singer lines in the west, extensions on-street could be made at Drumchapel, Milngavie and to Airdrie town centre, along with a new branch from Springburn to Balornock and a branch from the Airdrie line to Easterhouse. The frequent and busy services to Helensburgh and Balloch, along with the infrequent trains for the West Highland line, would have to be displaced to the Central low level line, already operating at near capacity. Additional tracks would have to be laid between Partick and Hyndland and there would have therefore to be some demolition of property in that area.

As this plan could have brought opposition to the scheme, an alternative strategy of five street based lines was also suggested. These lines were:

A To Drumchapel via a disused rail alignment and tunnel to Kirklee then via Great Western Road, using the former tram reservation.

B To Barmulloch and Balornock, on street via Springburn.

C To Easterhouse via disused rail lines to Edinburgh Road then on central reservation.

A link to Springburn and line B via Alexandra Parade would also be possible.

D A line from Bridgeton to Tollcross via a disused rail alignment.

E A line along the north bank of the Clyde to Kelvinbridge.

This alternative plan for the northern area was preferred and the estimated capital cost was £220 million. The central terminus would be a loop around Renfield Street, Argyle Street, Queen Street and Renfrew Street and some inter-running with the southern line would be possible. The report was illustrated with photographs of the then-new low floor trams of Grenoble, but high platform operation was also mentioned as a possibility.

In April 1990 the Council of the Region endorsed these plans, no doubt encouraged by a consultation exercise which showed that 60% of those interviewed were in favour of light rail, even though 52% of the sample had access to a car. After further work on the proposals had been carried out, a further consultation booklet, 'Travelling in Strathclyde' and a progress report were published in 1992. The local bus operators had been lobbying for guided buses and a study of these had been commissioned in 1991 from JMP Consultants, a firm known to be enthusiastic about these. It was not surprising that these now received more favourable notice for routes with passenger loading up to 2,500 passengers per hour, provided that no tunnel sections were involved. However, the general conclusion was favourable to light rail and it was stated that priority should be given to the northern lines. After yet more financial appraisal and a cost-benefit analysis, definite proposals for a line which would be a combination of lines 3C and 3E above were published for consultation in August 1994. Further studies continued on the other sections of this scheme.

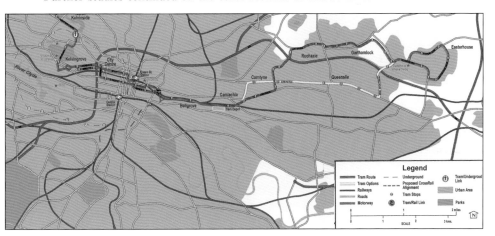

The final plan, for what was now called line 1 of the Strathclyde Tram, envisaged a line which would run as shown on the map. The terminal loop at Maryhill, would be on what was then a vacant area adjacent to a shopping centre. The form of one-way working chosen for the city centre was an engineer's solution, devised by the Region's Roads Department and was far from ideal from the passengers' point of view, as both lines would be separated by several blocks and would also be at different levels. There would be interchange with the Subway

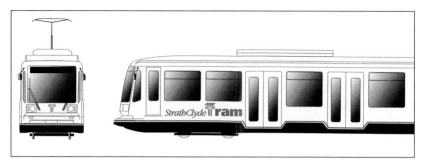

at Buchanan Street and with the main line services at Queen Street and High Street, where the lines would come together again and join the railway alignment to Parkhead Forge, where another new shopping centre would afford a useful amount of traffic. There was a choice of route from here via Edinburgh Road or Carntyne Road to Easterhouse, the latter alignment being that which was eventually chosen. At Easterhouse the line would terminate in a loop through the large estate of council houses, in which 86% of households in a population of 82,000 did not then have access to a car. Total length of the line was 20km and the depot was to be situated on derelict railway land at Camlachie in the inner east end of the city, not far from the former Dennistoun Depot of Glasgow Corporation. It was planned that there would be between 40 and 45 stops in total, six of which would have park and ride facilities. Stops would be 500m apart in the central area and about 1km apart elsewhere. These would have platforms of between 300mm and 400mm in height, providing level access to the trams. The basic service would have been a tram every ten minutes.

Publicity material showed low floor trams of a design almost identical to those of Sheffield, some even sporting the former Sheffield cream and blue livery, others a rather bland blue and white colour scheme. Rather strangely there was no attempt to harness the affection many citizens still had for the former trams by using some combination of orange, green and cream as a livery. The cars would have been double-articulated units with eight axles, 35m long and either 2.3m or 2.65m wide and with a total capacity of 250 passengers. The gauge chosen was 1435mm.

The service was expected to cover its running costs by a comfortable margin, with annual patronage running at about 15 million passengers. There would be a fairly high impact on urban regeneration, especially in Easterhouse. Apart from the passage under the M8 motorway at Blochairn, there would be little adverse impact on other traffic or public utilities and the general noise level would be low. Visually the line would not be intrusive, but there would be some loss of trees in Great Western Road and careful attention would have to be given to the impact on the flora and fauna along the bank of the River Kelvin.

This was an imaginative plan, which, had all gone well, would have seen trams return to Glasgow in 2002. Funding would be sought from what was then the Scottish Office, the EU and the private sector and it was intended that there would be a design, build, operate and maintain contract for the system. Some initial concern was expressed by Strathclyde Police about street running and there was some wider concern about the use of Kelvingrove Park, but in general the proposals were very well received. A further consultation exercise showed that light rail was supported by 88% of respondents and 79% preferred it to guided buses.

An exhibition, which also included plans for rail lines, was held in the city centre between August and October 1994, supplemented by five local displays along the line of route. The central exhibition attracted about 200 visitors per day and comments, not least from the then managing director of Celtic FC, were generally favourable. These exhibitions were supported by the publication of a series of leaflets describing the proposed route in detail, with the help of some excellent aerial photographs. Other leaflets dealt with issues of security and accessibility. At all stages the advantages of the trams for people with mobility impairments were stressed. The first of a planned series of newsletters also appeared – there were no further issues.

In 1995 the firm of MVA Consultancy was appointed to carry out an economic appraisal of both the Strathclyde Tram scheme and the Crossrail scheme which was also part of the plans for Glasgow. An environmental impact statement was also published, with an appendix and this also appeared as a non-technical summary, illustrated by a photograph of a Manchester car and, curiously, also by a view of a Glasgow Cunarder operating with a trolley pole in Blackpool in 1985.

REJECTION

In the same year a draft provisional order was deposited under the little-used Private Legislation Procedure (Scotland) Act of 1936. It was necessary to adopt this method as the Transport and Works Act of 1992 did not apply to Scotland. Parliamentary commissioners then went on to hold a public enquiry and, after this was concluded, they announced in June 1996 that the scheme was to be rejected. The commissioners were not obliged to, and chose not to, give any reason for their decision. Strathclyde Region had by this date been abolished, against the wishes of most of its inhabitants, and the boundaries drawn for the replacement authorities appeared to have been deliberately framed to reduce the tax base of the city of Glasgow. It was therefore most unlikely that the new unitary authorities would be able to raise sufficient funding for their share of the costs and an additional amount of grant aid would have had to be sought from the Scottish Office. All this was carried out by a government which then had only a small minority of MPs in Scotland and which was one year later to lose all its representation in the country. Fortunately the PTE survived but was now bereft of the support of a strong regional authority. It was also by now poorer by the £2 million it had spent on preparation of the scheme. The only visible result of years of planning, consultation and the associated expenditure were the institution of a suburban service from Queen Street HL to Maryhill and the reopening of the suburban line to Coatbridge via Whifflet.

Given the secrecy in which the commissioners operated, the reasons for the rejection of what was a well-considered and thoroughly costed plan can only be guessed. It is likely that the choice of a route to Easterhouse may have played some part in this, since the trams would not have been able to attract many people away from car use – there not being many cars in Easterhouse – although it would certainly have played a key part in the regeneration of the area. Glasgow has, since bus deregulation, been subjected to many wars between competing operators, of which the main operator at the time, Strathclyde Buses, was certainly hostile to the idea of a tramway and suggested that it could provide an equivalent standard of service at much less cost, using some form of busway.

There were subsequent plans for some form of regional light rail network, some members of the PTE having visited Karlsruhe, from which they returned impressed. A light rail line to Glasgow Airport was discussed later in 1996 and, although it did not then find favour with rail user groups, it is not yet dead.

LEEDS

As patient crowds said their sad farewells to the trams in Leeds on a November day during 1959, few could have foreseen that trams would return. The rich variety of trams was quietly and quickly put to the torch and done with such haste that it tended to alert one's mind into questioning the wisdom of it all. Any potential question would no doubt take into consideration Leeds's bold initiative when, as late as 1949, a track link was provided between Middleton and Belle Isle, described in transport circles as the finest tramway ever built in Britain.

In 1952 two new and technically advanced railcars were added to the tram fleet. Part of the failure was a very poor passenger-staff ratio – no fault of the technical design, because the articulated tram at that time had not been success-fully applied in Europe. Another nail in the railcars' coffin came from the proposed city centre subways for which they had been experimentally provided. By now the possible construction of underground tramways had become an election issue, mainly due to the anticipated costs.

In 1977 consultants employed by the former West Yorkshire Metropolitan County Council suggested some early planning action for a tramway-type light rail system in Leeds. This suggestion though was not included in their final recommendations; it was probably too bold an initiative after less than a 20 year period since the trams disappeared. One must not forget that Britain then was at the height of its motorway era and this could have been interpreted as a challenge, no matter how unintentional, to the proud boast that Leeds was the motorway city of the 1970s.

The consultants took into account the approaching disposal of railway land as a follow onto the 'Beeching Axe'. This though would have created a dilemma because, in an urban context, suburban railway lines were not always located where a local passenger would wish to go. This the consultants resolved by offer-ing two alternative suggestions, one highway based and the other designed to utilise redundant railway formations.

By the late 1980s when grid-lock on the roads had become an almost daily occurrence, a City Council brochure revealed a forecast rise of 50% in traffic in the next ten years and that serious moves were necessary to find a workable transport solution. There was thought at this time to be a wide divergence of opinion between the City Council and the Public Transport Authority, which seemed to nullify any actual progress being made.

Being twinned with Lille in France, the City council looked at that city's new automated VAL rubber tyred transit system and decided that Leeds could benefit from something similar. At that time a similar British designed system with the trade name of BRIWAY was readily available but still seriously lacking in operational experience. Being untested, the City Council were taking a cal-culated risk in preparing a Bill for Parliament with BRIWAY as their preferred technology. Given the fancy name of LEEDS ADVANCED TRANSIT, or LAT for short, this partly elevated system was claimed to be capable of moving 10,000 people per hour in either direction. The cars would be fully automated, air con-ditioned and capable of 50 mph at a two-minute frequency during peak periods.

They would ride on rubber tyres along a concrete track and be capable of negotiating sharp bends and steep slopes when fully loaded. The cars would seat 20 with another 25 standing. With the total of 20 unmanned stations, lifts or escalators would be needed to reach them. Each passenger without a period ticket would be required to negotiate the automatic ticket machine on each platform. Although several routes were planned for this system, the first would have been 12 miles long and take 30 minutes for an end to end journey. Basically, the route would be from the east, through the city centre and then towards the south of the city. A series of fail-safe features would have included a battery back-up arrangement for emergency operation during a power failure.

Also being evaluated by Leeds City Council were the benefits of a guided bus network. Although capable of operating over special tracks segregated from other road traffic, they could rejoin the normal highway at road junctions in the suburbs and in the central area. Whilst capable of playing its part in the future of public transport in Leeds, it was realised that the guided bus concept alone could not solve the city's traffic problems. Nevertheless it does have the advantage of being able to reach all the outlying districts of Leeds at no extra cost. A report produced by the Leeds Civic Trust during September 1989 to specifically reply to the City Council on the various options being considered for a Parliamentary Bill made an important point about the questionnaire. It was noted that the LAT news broadsheet appeared as strongly biased in favour of the elevated LAT system at the expense of the guided bus, with the tram option dismissed out-of-hand. As the guided bus scheme developed, the concept passed into a private bus operator's hands and adopted a new name, BUS EXPRESS TRANSIT, shortened to BEST.

A 1990 brochure by Yorkshire Rider, the bus company now promoting BEST, indicated that it supported the light rail concept as an integral part of urban rapid transit. However it pointed out that light rail usually requires a lead time of several years for implementation, needs 'up-front' investment and the securing of special Parliamentary powers through an enabling act. Whenever a light rail transit scheme can be developed from major existing rail resources, such as suburban electric rail to a METROLINK type of operation, it is logical to develop it as light rail. Often that is not the case and that is where the bus-based BEST system can bring rapid, cheap and substantial benefit.

Not to be eclipsed by rubber tyred schemes, the West Yorkshire PTA put forward METROLINE, which was basically a tramway with cars that that were 2.65 metres wide and 27 metres long. Providing the necessary powers could be obtained, the line would start at the Town Hall, use the Headrow to reach York Road and then fan out to serve three destinations; Seacroft, Crossgates and Colton. Being 85% segregated from other traffic, and passing through some of the most densely populated areas of Leeds, it was claimed as environmentally friendly and with no requirement to demolish any homes. This £38 million, 12km scheme, with 170 passenger trams, was expected to draw the necessary funding from three sources, 40% from Central Government, 40% from West Yorkshire PTA and 20% from the private sector. Several difficulties, some of major significance, 'dogged' this METROLINE proposal and one serious difficulty, highlighted by the City Council, was its failure to connect with the Railway Station. Another problem which had some political overtones was a strip of land in the Colton area. This had now become a 'residual asset' and once sold, when the County Council was disbanded, would play a major part in killing off the Colton section of the scheme.

More positive was the attitude of the Chamber of Trade and the Kirkgate Market Traders Association who are on record in the 1991 Leeds Transport Strategy Summary as welcoming a policy of supporting road schemes where they reduce the amount of through traffic in the city centre. They also supported the need for more short stay parking for shoppers. They were extremely concerned though that the Government might only offer funding for an experimental guided bus route, regarded by them as an inferior system which will not in any way tackle congestion or promote a new image for the city.

With so many city centre roads at a standstill almost daily, the local railway services now came under close scrutiny. With such a tremendous potential tied up in the suburban network, the message coming out of the Wharfedale line to Ilkley made dismal reading with commuters on that line holding protest meetings in the hope of stopping the threatened cuts to their services. The Bradford service in particular was to lose its direct link from Ilkley. The corollary of this was a consultants' report to the West Yorkshire PTA recommending a light rail service from Leeds to Ilkley and include a branch to serve the Leeds and Bradford Airport at Yeadon. This branch would also include a connection to the Leeds to Harrogate line at Horsforth. Although the proposals were accepted by the PTA, they were short lived because the then British Rail decided to electrify the Ilkley Line at main line voltage. This move appeared to be connected with a decision to stop Intercity services from Kings Cross via Leeds to Bradford calling at New Pudsey and to change to the Airedale route, a change which permitted electric Intercity trains to reach Skipton. The significance of this was that the branch to Ilkley gained a suburban electric service but lost any possibility of being connected to future Supertram services in Leeds and the potential link to the bus station.

Just as METROLINE was a disguised name for light rail, ELECTROBUS was an equally disguised name for a trolleybus when it first appeared in a 1980s West Yorkshire PTA brochure. The first new West Yorkshire trolleybus installation would have been a 39km route in Leeds requiring 44 vehicles to connect Moortown and Roundhay in north Leeds with Middleton and Cottingley in the south. A small auxiliary diesel engine would have permitted emergency operation when away from the wires. The second phase would have been an isolated route in Bradford followed by a link between the two systems as phase three. Because bus deregulation was likely to make trolleybus operation vulnerable to competition, Government decided to delay a financial package.

It could be said that in transit terms, the 1980s had been disastrous for Leeds. The LAT BRIWAY scheme had failed to attract public support, the METROLINE light rail scheme had failed to attract City Council support, the METROLINE Bill in Parliament was withdrawn and lastly, the trolleybus proposals had failed to attract Government support. The guided bus project was the only urban scheme to escape unscathed and eventually it passed its final obstacle when the section along the Scott Hall Road corridor opened in 1995. Much controversy has surrounded the operator's claims of patronage success and recently published data has suggested that increases in patronage are not so much attributed to the guided bus itself but to service rationalisation and elimination of competitors.

It was now back to the drawing board for both the City Council and the PTA but with some additional help coming from the Leeds Development Corporation. By this time the public had become somewhat disillusioned at the apparent lack of progress. In an attempt to break the deadlock, a new joint working party was commissioned to settle proposals for an agreed transport strategy. In order to come up with something acceptable to all parties, the joint working party awarded contracts to two consultants: Steer, Davies and Gleave to develop the model for the city, and Ove Arup Associates to examine the proposed Leeds alignments. By now it was time for a public consultation exercise, which was launched early in 1991 to consider and approve funding allocations. These were £250 million for Supertram, £100 million for roads, £170 million for buses and railways and £100 million for traffic management.

With all-party support, a Bill for an 11.25km Supertram system requiring 22 trams was lodged late in 1991. This was for a line from Cookridge Street in Leeds city centre to a major park-and-ride terminal at Tingley with a small branch from Hunslet to Stourton, again terminating at a park-and-ride site. Although Royal Assent was granted during July 1993, and a successful bidder selected very shortly afterwards, the project could not proceed further because at that time funding was simply not available. The successful bidder had been Eurotrans which was a consortium made up of British Bus, Vevey Technologies, Taylor Woodrow, Christiani & Nielson and Morrison Construction. Without any movement on the project for a number of years, both the Supertram project and the appointed consortium had experienced some major changes which in effect meant a completely new tendering process for a much expanded system.

The mere existence of a Supertram plan was more an act of faith by the City Council and the PTA because both had been under extreme pressure to change to something less ambitious. To keep the Supertram project alive, a technique resembling 'horse trading' was employed. This was an offer to conduct trials for road charging but with an understanding that it must be in the best interests of the city and that a viable public transport alternative to the car was already in place. This created a potential for some political squabbling, fortunately avoided when the Government dropped its requirement of some 'up-front' congestion charging and offered a generous funding package towards Supertram. This may have been influenced by a local newspaper indicating public opposition of 30 to 1 against the road toll concept.

When the powers to build Supertram lapsed in 1998, all local political parties showed determination to retain the Supertram concept by agreeing to renew the powers with just a few small changes. This went before the full City Council for support from its members and a subsequent vote showed unanimous approval. Despite a funding log-jam from a long and cool attitude by Central Government towards light rail schemes in general, a local decision considerably extended the planned network by adding a north-west branch to Boddington (Lawnswood) and a north-east branch to Whinmoor (Seacroft). As for the city centre, the concept of a tramway ring around the shopping core was agreed on. This transport box in the city centre has been designed to take people as close as possible to places of popular demand. This box will be mostly of double track, but in a few narrow streets will be one-way single track.

The contentious nature of some of the extensions called for a public inquiry which, with Sir Norman King KBE as inspector, was held during March and April 1997. The judgement was eventually released late in 2000 and displayed a very positive approach to Supertram and some encouraging comments from the Inspector. He noted that whilst objectors did not accept that Supertram would meet the objectives set, there was a general acceptance by the Leeds Transport Strategy. Little doubt remained that each point raised during the inquiry had been thoroughly investigated. For instance, any noise coming from Supertram would be less than from other large vehicles such as buses and lorries.

Safety was likely to be improved overall for all road users. Supertram would be more cost effective than an enhanced bus provision. A loss of public space or trees should be accepted for the greater public benefit of the scheme and tree replacement would replace lost trees. Construction traffic will be routed by heavy goods vehicles routes and traffic calming will be investigated to reduce rat running. There is no evidence that Supertram would in general reduce the value of properties alongside or close to the route.

Funding to build the project was included in the Ten Year Transport Investment Programme but was less than clear-cut during the initial stages. One prime reason for this was a need for the project to pass the Government's recent value-for-money appraisal. Of the three priority bands, the first consisted of fully approved projects and was made up of only road schemes. The second was for schemes accepted but not fully approved whilst the third was for schemes yet to be evaluated against this new appraisal procedure. Although Leeds is in this last band, a positive result seems assured. The scheme now is a 28km project costed at £487 million pounds and requiring 40 trams, each capable of carrying 270 passengers. 75% of the network will be segregated and expected to be attractive enough to attract among its passengers 25% of former car users. The four park-and-ride sites are designated to hold a total of 4900 cars which should contribute towards an estimated modal change adding up to a reduction of 64 million-kms per year.

Nearly 100 firms were present to show an interest in bidding for this 30-year design, build, operate and maintain contract when the official launch took place during June 2001. The actual bidding should start early in 2002 with the mainstream construction scheduled to commence late in 2003. Completion date is targeted for 2007. Already being proposed is a feasibility study into extending the network into outlying areas such as Leeds and Bradford Airport, Wakefield, Huddersfield, Halifax and Bradford.

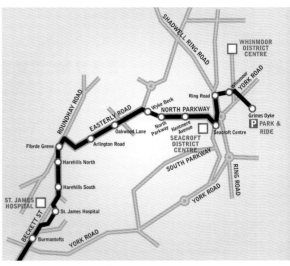

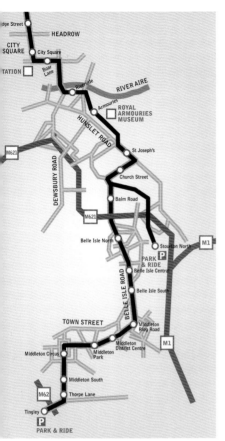

Left **Stage 1 of the Leeds Supertram will run from Cookridge Street to Tingley.**

Below **Stage 2 is planned to run between the City Centre and a park and ride site on the A660 at Bodington. It will provide a service to the universities.**

Above **Stage 3 links the City Centre with Whinmoor.**

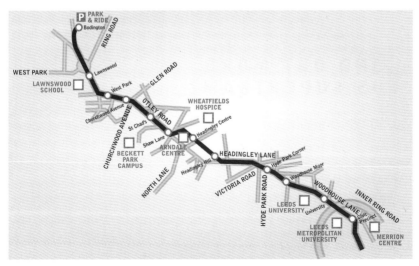

How a tram might look on Waterloo Bridge.

LONDON

London once had an extremely large conventional tramway system, the origins of which could be said to have emerged from Mr Train's short lived Bayswater Road horse line of 1861. Much has been written about London's first generation tramway elsewhere, so only this short note is required here to recognise its former existence. Although some minor lines disappeared in the earlier years of the 20th century, most of the former municipal, private company and London County Council tramways were absorbed into London Transport's tramway system in 1933. Trams reached suburban extremities including Barnet and Waltham Cross in the north, Uxbridge in the west, Purley in the south and Chadwell Heath and Horns Cross to the east. The most obvious peculiarity highlighted by study of a map of the tramway network at its peak was the hole in the centre of the system, caused by the refusal of Westminster Council and the City of London to permit the installation of logical tramway connections across the heart of London, thus denying the capital of trams on what could have been the busiest tram routes had they ever been created. There was one notable exception – using a feature unique on UK's first generation tramways – the Kingsway tram subway. The other special feature, almost unique in the UK, was the employment of long sections of conduit powered tramway, mainly through the inner suburbs, imposed as a condition by local councils who did not want the skyline disturbed by overhead wires. Change pits appeared at numerous locations where trams shot their plough to adopt overhead power collection allowed on outer sections and this exercise became a fascinating feature of tramway operation in the capital unique in the UK. Tramway abandonment started in earnest in 1935, with final closure of the system in July 1952.

Whilst Croydon Tramlink is the only modern tram system in London at present, street running was part of early plans for the Docklands Light Railway. Different schemes envisaged street running along parts of Burdett Road, Mile End Road and the Commercial Road before the decision for an automatic railway made full-segregation from road traffic essential.

ADDINGTON AUTOMATIC PEOPLEMOVER

It had long been realised that New Addington, created from the late 1930s onwards with very limited self sufficiency as a dormitory on an isolated hillside some 5 miles south east of Croydon, was London's largest centre of population without a rail link. Initially, the developers supported a special temporary bus link to Croydon, with Addington's long standing public transport lifeline to the outside world starting up on 5th July 1939. This was London Transport's 130 bus route, which despite variations at both ends, has been the core service into the vast estate until the introduction of Tramlink, retaining concentrated levels of service, long since lost from suburban local routes elsewhere in London, as well as complementary Express variants at peak hours.

In 1974, the Greater London Council examined the possibilities of providing the missing rail link into Addington. It commissioned a feasibility study of various new driverless automatic transport systems, carried out by a consortium of consultants, managed by a steering group containing representatives from LT and the London Borough of Croydon and the GLC. However, the scope of the examination, although keen to utilise the latest technology to satisfy this need, was actually rather narrow. There was an obsession with applying what was perceived as futuristic peoplemover technology to the problem, envisaging an automated railway on totally segregated lines running between Addington and Croydon. The peoplemover concept, sometimes referred to as minitrams, would have called for small rail-based driverless vehicles, holding up to about 20 people each, running at high frequencies. The novel modes studied were: GEC Easams Minitram, Hawker-Siddeley Minitram, Otis Elevator Hovair, the Matra 'VAL', the Habegger Minirail and the Hitachi-ALWEG Monorail. These modes were assessed, routes suggested and evaluation drawn against bus improvement options. From the conclusions published in 1976, it was clear that the study had grasped the need for a mass-mover rail link and accepted that demand was not likely to justify a long extension of a tube railway. Because it was wedded to an automatic line requiring a suitable totally segregated corridor which proved to be unavailable at the Croydon end, the idea was shelved.

The Addington study made the sad error of asking the wrong question. It was system-led rather than demand-led. It started with a solution and then sought ways of proving it, which because it was an inappropriate solution to the problem it failed to find that proof. There was no freedom to study the problem with an open ended choice of solutions available. The tramway option was only briefly considered then and thought to have little advantage over buses, whereas later studies have shown that a partially segregated light rail scheme can be feasible. Also, it was not surprising that traffic levels could not justify the high cost of largely elevated structures and stations necessary to achieve full segregation for an automatic system, or that they were environmentally unacceptable in a mixed urban and wooded area.

THE RUNNACLES REPORT

In April 1977, Tim Runnacles, then of the Transport Strategy section within London Transport's Planning Office, produced a discussion paper entitled *An Exploratory Study of Light Rail Transit and Modern Tramways in Greater London*. The document makes interesting reading today and, whilst wide of the mark in some areas, it is surprisingly accurate and relevant to today's more enlightened light rail thinking.

This internal document argued for a light rail study to be undertaken, and suggested possible corridors in considerable detail. The opening paragraph high-lights the lack of any serious proposal to examine light rail up to that time, but mentions a contemporary superficial study into transport in Docklands, and a Croydon to New Addington study. Runnacles then reveals that 'In both cases, the tramway solutions were rejected'. The recommended Docklands solution of the time was to be a deep level tube line, for many years referred to as the Fleet Line with a later variant taking in Woolwich and Thamesmead, adopting the *River Line* tag. Croydon to Addington had been rejected for light rail because: 'difficulties would have been encountered in finding suitable routes for bring-ing tracks into Croydon'.

The Addington line, as already mentioned, was not to have been a conven-tional tramway in today's sense, but rather an automatic people mover with driverless minitrams utilising viaducts and requiring a fully segregated right of way. In 1976 it would have been heresy to dare to suggest the idea of sharing the streets with other traffic, and to challenge the total freedom enjoyed by the private motor car. Even where the tram continued to find favour during the 1960s and 1970s on the European mainland, the only way of ensuring its sur-vival was to keep the tram away from the motor car by segregating its tracks at all costs rather than curtail the freedom of the motor car in cities. In some cities large sums of money were invested in tunnels to hide the tram away, often with pre-metro construction which allowed eventual transition into a heavy metro to replace the trams altogether. Only as we moved into the 1990s came the really radical acceptance that efficient public transport must be fast and free from traffic delays, but at the same time easily accessible to its users who usually arrive on foot. To achieve this, private car restraint has to be accepted, and this is now beginning to happen. Runnacles could see this as long ago as 1977, but he was then a lone voice. Runnacles also recognised that in many circumstances it would be more economical to operate a tracked system under driver control rather than investing in high tech automatic systems. The first strands of reviving this line of thought were in embryonic form elsewhere, with exploratory studies under way in cities like Edinburgh, Sheffield, Liverpool and Manchester.

The 1977 document based its plea for serious study on the subject of light rail for London on very sound reasoning. It was concerned about the escalating costs of oil, as well as the case for reducing manpower costs in public transport operation. (The 1970s were a period of plentiful employment prospects in the South East, and in an attempt to reduce staff shortages, higher pay rates for public transport workers were the order of the day.) The planks of the argument are mainly still relevant in support of light rail today, although there has been a slight shift of emphasis during the intervening changing industrial climate, whilst the argument for change to electricity as the power source has moved from a cost issue to an environmental one.

Runnacles examined all of the roles which light rail could fulfil, ranging from conventional street tramway with traffic management and tram priorities through semi- and pre-metro states to conversion to heavy rail or metro, and also automatic minitram. He visualised opportunities in London for replacing high volume bus corridors with modern tramways, mainly using street track with traffic priorities and short subway sections to avoid major traffic junctions. The other source for new tramway was seen as being as an alternative to new underground lines, and converting suburban sections of existing heavy rail lines, feeding these onto street sections as appropriate to improve penetration to town centres. He calculated that to construct and equip every mile of new underground railway costed almost five times that of surface tramway. How far-sighted he was.

His first idea was sparked off by the then recent developments in cities which had started to reverse tram abandonment plans, such as Amsterdam. The main spur for this action derived from labour shortages and costs, and the important fact that the carrying capacity per crew member of a modern tram was far in excess of that of a bus. It was also interesting to note that where trams had replaced buses, they had attracted increased patronage over the routes concerned. The report identified corridors in London carrying more than 40 buses per hour in the peak. It demonstrated that where peak hour flows exceeded 1400 passengers, tram operation, despite its infrastructure requirements, could start to become more economical than the bus. True, some of the priority measures could be adopted by buses as well as trams, and this pushed the viability edge of tram over bus to a 6100 passengers per peak hour threshold.

The report identified the key *bus replacement* tram corridors for street tramways in London as shown in the map below, and offered suggestions for carrying these across the central area, using some subways and semi metro corridors to achieve this. Not surprisingly, the Kingsway Subway featured in his plans.

Some lines were suggested reincarnations of former trunk tram routes (e.g. the 16/18 along Brighton Road to Purley). The study was extensive, and it is fascinating to see from the maps overleaf how complex track junction layouts at places like Marble Arch were envisaged. One day, maybe it will prove even more fascinating to compare these plans with the reality?

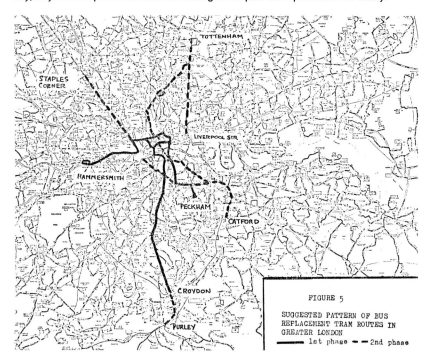

FIGURE 5

SUGGESTED PATTERN OF BUS REPLACEMENT TRAM ROUTES IN GREATER LONDON

—— 1st phase — — 2nd phase

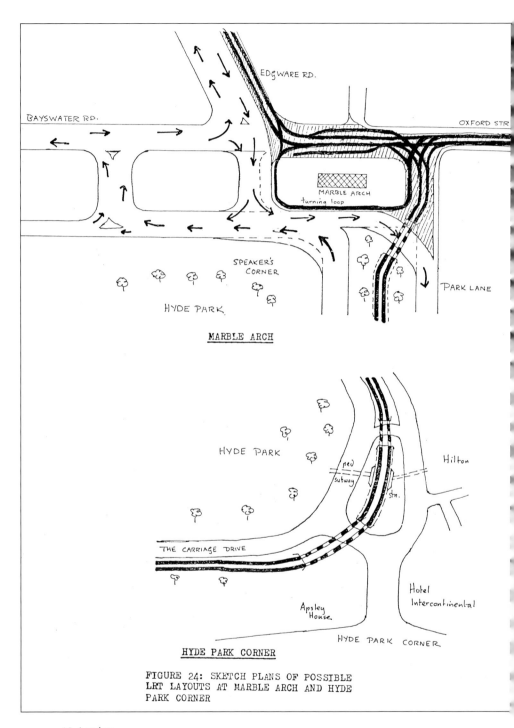

MARBLE ARCH

HYDE PARK CORNER

FIGURE 24: SKETCH PLANS OF POSSIBLE
LRT LAYOUTS AT MARBLE ARCH AND HYDE
PARK CORNER

Whilst he remarks on the lack of any rival to the River Line plan to serve Docklands, the second category of tram possibilities probed by Runnacles suggests a surface tramway alternative to the proposed Chelsea–Hackney tube line. This philosophy was given a sub-chapter of its own, and started from the base that Chelsea–Hackney was a new tube to relieve parts of the Victoria and Central lines and designed also to serve parts of north-east inner London which were without a tube service. There were a number of variants on the route, and there have been further since, but the common thread at the time was to adopt the southern end of the District Line between Wimbledon and Fulham Broadway, diving underground there to serve a new station at Chelsea Town Hall. Continuation underground was to take the new line via Sloane Square, Victoria, Piccadilly Circus, Tottenham Court Road, Kings Cross, Angel, Essex Road, Dalston Junction, Hackney Central, Homerton. The likely route from here would be on the surface to Leytonstone from which point the new line would take over the Hainault branch of the Central Line.

The report suggested that in theoretical terms, it would be possible to use light rail as an alternative to the Chelsea–Hackney line, and that a surface alternative with street running could be built for about 25 per cent of the cost. It was recognised that freedom from hindrance would have to be ensured to enable surface running. Whilst it was noted that speed and capacity would be a little below that of the proposed Underground line, the improved accessibility that street running would provide for the user over the need to descend to the bowels of the earth to catch the tube was seen as good compensation for these factors.

The detail talked of some private right of way being used near BR marshalling yards at Temple Mills, and of short stretches of subway construction at Fulham and in Hackney, but most of the light rail alternative was to use almost 10 miles of street track.

The idea of adopting the ends of the District and Central lines and converting these to light rail was part of the Runnacles plan, although it recognised the need to use the Epping rather than the Hainault branch if light rail vehicles were to be used. Runnacles discussed the problems of light rail alongside heavy rail, and the possibility of track sharing, and related this to the situation in Frankfurt-am-Main where this concept had been in place for some time by 1977. He contrasted the accurate timetabling adherence possible on a segregated railway with the more random result expected from a street system, and was therefore only luke warm towards the idea of incorporating the District/ Central portions of the scheme into the light rail alternative.

The third tramway opportunity – that of downgrading certain suburban sections of BR and the Underground – looked at seven examples: Catford to Addiscombe, Hayes and Sanderstead; Wimbledon to Streatham; Purley to Caterham; Purley to Tattenham Corner; Epsom Downs to Sutton; Wimbledon to Sutton via St Helier; and West Croydon to Wimbledon via Mitcham. Most of these were subjected to further serious evaluation by LT in their 1986 work, but it is most interesting to read that Runnacles should select sections which were later to become parts of Tramlink, and to read his belief that '... A street tramway link could also be built from Addiscombe Station via East Croydon to West Croydon, thereby providing not only a useful round the corner link but also enhancing the value of Croydon as a focal point of a new light rail network'. The new scheme used Bingham Road rather than Addiscombe, but did Tim Runnacles have a crystal ball before him back in 1977?

Combining all three philosophies for tramway revival, his system totalled 131 miles of tramway for London.

Runnacles then goes on to examine the physical accommodation and design standards of possible modern tramways in London. Several alternative drawings show how segregated and integrated tramway alignments could fit into different street widths, and considerable attention is paid to the optimum siting of stops. He even dared to suggest that the difficulty with non-segregated tracks in the centre of the carriageway could be overcome by tram-actuated traffic signal protection whilst passengers board and alight.

Following a conclusion chapter which sums up the major findings described here, the report closes after a range of appendices which apply mathematics to the assumptions made and list light rail systems around the world at that time. Most fascinating however is the drawing of a suggested coupled pair of double deck tramcars, resembling updates of the erstwhile Swansea – Mumbles giants, compared to a DMS bus and a Feltham tram. An adjoining table suggests a length per car of 17 metres and a carrying capacity of 222 in each. At that point, perhaps the Runnacles crystal ball has clouded over a little?

Although the Runnacles paper evoked considerable interest, it failed to shift London Transport's emphasis from heavy metro planning and high density bus coverage. There was a very strong belief at Executive level that where a full metro line was unjustified, the bus was the only proper solution. The report was visionary and in many ways, years ahead of contemporary UK thinking.

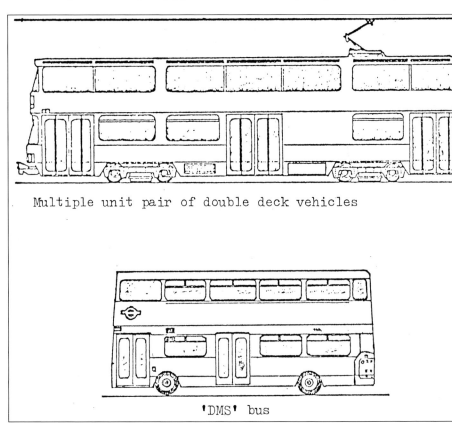

Multiple unit pair of double deck vehicles

'DMS' bus

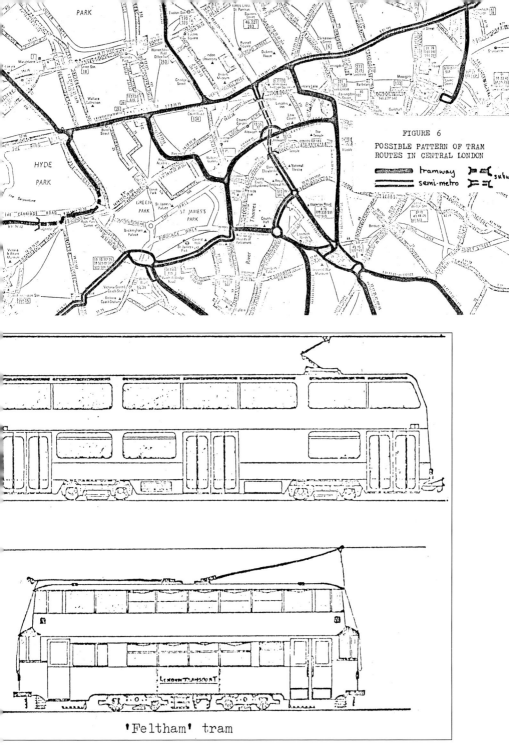

FIGURE 6

POSSIBLE PATTERN OF TRAM
ROUTES IN CENTRAL LONDON

tramway

semi-metro

subway

'Feltham' tram

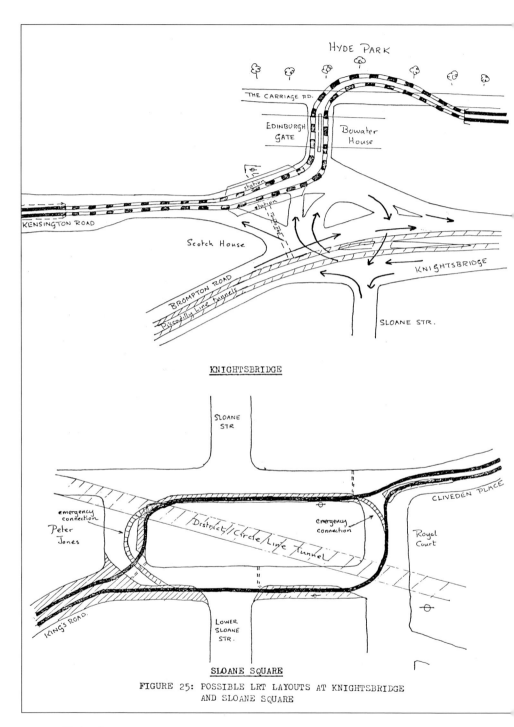

FIGURE 25: POSSIBLE LRT LAYOUTS AT KNIGHTSBRIDGE
AND SLOANE SQUARE

1979: POSSIBLE LRT APPLICATIONS IN LONDON

Not all of the Runnacles seeds fell on stony ground, however. In the climate of the time, it was nothing short of remarkable that the LT Board was even willing to consider intermediate modes at all. David Catling was appointed as LT's first Engineering Manager (New Rail Systems) in 1979. A small team within LT railways examined possible sites in the London area in the categories suggested by the Runnacles report. It was also to look further into the concept of Automatic Light Rail Transit (ALRT) as a cheaper form of underground railway. Amongst studies to spring from this initiative were:

⋄ Evaluation of Minitram along A23 corridor – April 1979.
⋄ Feasibility Study for Peoplemover Link between Hatton Cross and Terminal 4 – November 1979.
⋄ Preliminary Feasibility Study for a low cost light rail link between Finsbury Park & Muswell Hill – December 1980.

EVALUATION OF MINITRAM ALONG A23 CORRIDOR – APRIL 1979

This report concluded that there could be a case for substituting elevated minitrams along the most heavily bussed corridors, but if the overhead structures proved to be environmentally unacceptable, the sub-surface options would almost certainly be too expensive. It recommended that technical work should be undertaken into guided systems for possible application at some later date when, as the trend was seen to be at that time, the costs and availability of labour employed in bus operation reached a more critical level. It was also recognised that other factors, such as the price and availability of fuel oil, or future volumes of traffic congestion, might hold sway on the future merit of ALRT.

Subsequently, a computer model was developed to determine precise levels of traffic demand required to justify the construction of various forms of Automatic Light Rail Transit. This could also forecast the likelihood of extra patronage, and optimise the combined effect of ALRT and other modes. This work revealed that ALRT would generally be worth consideration at surface level where 40 or more buses per hour were currently in peak operation. However, if elevated structures were needed, the viability threshold was pushed upwards by 125 per cent, whilst to contemplate underground operation of minitrams this rose to 350 per cent. Thus the most promising corridors for even surface schemes were limited, with examples including the southern end of the Edgware Road, and part of the A23 (Oval to Streatham). The report also recognised that ALRT might also be relevant to parts of the Chelsea–Hackney alignment.

FEASIBILITY STUDY FOR PEOPLEMOVER LINK BETWEEN HATTON CROSS AND TERMINAL 4 – NOVEMBER 1979

This work examined the possibility of installing a fully automatic guideway transit peoplemover system between Hatton Cross station and Heathrow Terminal 4 as an alternative to construction of the proposed Piccadilly Line extension. BAA had changed the location of the site for the proposed Terminal 4, and this now meant that the Piccadilly Line was pointing the wrong way to serve it conventionally. There was however only limited time available within the British Airports Authority programme to allow for all the necessary planning, legal and environmental issues to be addressed, and so a tube extension in the form of a unidirectional loop went ahead without full assessment of the alternative.

PRELIMINARY FEASIBILITY STUDY FOR A LOW COST LIGHT RAIL LINK BETWEEN FINSBURY PARK & MUSWELL HILL – DECEMBER 1980.

The main purpose of this study was to pull together ideas for reviving part of a former British Railways line which had closed in 1954. This line, from Finsbury Park to Highgate, and then across to Alexandra Palace had once formed part of London Transport's ambitious 1935 New Works programme. It was planned that the Northern City Line between Moorgate and Finsbury Park be diverted from Drayton Park to electrify and take over existing BR tracks through Finsbury Park to Alexandra Palace. The same programme would also have provided for services from Moorgate to split at Highgate to feed what became the Mill Hill East branch of the Northern Line and extend beyond that point to Edgware and Bushey Heath. Despite the considerable works that had taken place along the route, this entire scheme was abandoned. The track from East Finchley through Highgate surface level platforms to Drayton Park had remained in use for stock movements until 1970, whilst the trackbed over most of the section between Park Junction (immediately north of Highgate north tunnel) and Alexandra Palace remained in use as a parkland walk.

The route presented a promising case study on which to examine more closely the potential of a low cost light rail line for London. A major remit was to decide whether a scheme on part of this line might look sufficiently promising to justify an initial approach to Haringey Council to sound out their interest and likely support. It might then be feasible to use this as a proving ground for British industry to try out low-cost technologies and operating practices.

The potential of this proposal could bear fruit in a number of ways. A service along this line, which wound its quiet path through hilly terrain and avoided the heavily congested streets in the area, could provide a regular, more economical and speedier service than the high-density bus services that then linked (and still do link) Muswell Hill to Highgate and Finsbury Park. The line lies in an area which falls between the Northern and Piccadilly lines which was now devoid of its direct rail service. It was also important to maintain the very pleasant nature of the trackbed, and light rail had the capability of fulfilling this. A map of the proposed light rail line is shown overleaf.

Under this proposal for a 5.77km line, Muswell Hill would be the likely northern terminus with double track. This would reduce to single to share the viaduct, blessed with impressive views across London, with the woodland walk. Double track would resume before Cranley Gardens station, continuing through to Stroud Green via the former railway line, with minor deviation to avoid more recent obstacles as necessary. Unlike the old railway which had crossed over the main Great Northern tracks, the light rail proposal was to take a new elevated single track alignment west of these to terminate at new high level platforms on the west side of Finsbury Park BR station. In addition to the former BR stations, light rail would have additional stops at Park Junction, Stanhope Road, Mountview Road. In addition to the use of light rail standards, and lighter track (60lb per yard rail) metre gauge was suggested rather than 1435mm. Power would be by overhead contact wire, and 'basic' signalling would be supplied only to protect single track sections. Elsewhere, tramway 'line of sight' driving would prevail. Stations would be unmanned, and two car light trains or articulated trams were suggested as rolling stock. All in all a modest construction cost was estimated to be £16m.

In discussing the possible benefits of such a scheme, the analysis took into account some saving from bus reductions upon transfer of traffic. However, the conclusion of the study was that the optimum operational value of the line would be around £400,000 per year, which was said to justify a capital outlay of only some £7m, well short of the estimated construction costs of the light rail line on this path. There was therefore no economic case to proceed with the proposal, unless special funding arrangements could be made on the grounds of the project becoming a research and development testbed. Other snags which weighed against this scheme included the need to move an old people's home which existed on the alignment, and proposals to widen the A1 which could have encroached on the alignment. Alas this potential light rail pioneer failed to materialise.

Later in the 1980s, frustrated by LT's failure to develop the light rail scheme for this line, a local group known as the Muswell Hill Metro Group put forward further proposals at lower cost, including suggestions to introduce light rail from Muswell Hill via Alexandra Palace grounds and on via Station Road to Wood Green. Without the support of Haringey Council, and opposed by the conservation lobby, this idea also came to nought.

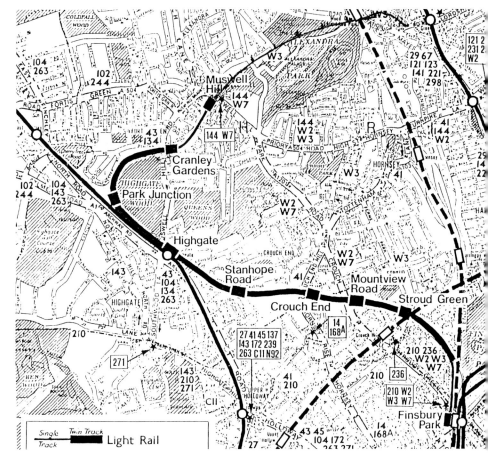

1986 'LIGHT RAIL FOR LONDON ?'

This joint BR/LT study identified scope for the application of light rail in around 40 possible schemes. It did not envisage a widescale introduction of light rail schemes because of the existing dense conventional rail network around London. However, it did see light rail as an infiller, replacing some of the less well patronised lines and connecting up a few loose ends by introducing limited street running. An important benefit was cost cutting to save otherwise vulnerable sections of line from possible extinction. Methodology would include the addition of extra stops, lower capital renewal costs and destaffing. It did not foresee a significant revenue improvement.

The schemes examined fell into three categories: conversion of heavy rail with or without extension, new routes to serve inner and outer London developments, and conversion of major bus corridors.

The following were suggested as direct conversions from conventional to light rail, with no suggestions of extension or street running. Where not electrified, these lines would have been so equipped, and in some cases, extra stops might have been proposed also. The report carried health warnings on many of these, stating that careful assessment of the penalty of additional interchange would need to be made. It also saw problems in segregating lines from the main rail network in most cases.

- ✧ Gospel Oak to Barking
- ✧ East London Line, plus extension into Liverpool Street via BR tracks
- ✧ Stratford to North Woolwich (possibly being taken over by DLR)
- ✧ Woodford to Ongar and Hainault replacing Central Line
- ✧ Romford to Upminster
- ✧ Blackheath to Slade Green via Bexleyheath
- ✧ Grove Park to Bromley North
- ✧ Purley to Caterham
- ✧ West Croydon to Wimbledon via Mitcham
- ✧ West Croydon to Wimbledon via Sutton
- ✧ South London Line (Victoria to London Bridge, plus new service Clapham Junction to Lewisham)
- ✧ Peckham Rye to Wimbledon via Streatham
- ✧ Sydenham to Herne Hill via West Norwood
- ✧ Sydenham to Balham via West Norwood
- ✧ Streatham to Epsom via Mitcham Junction and Sutton
- ✧ Raynes Park to Epsom
- ✧ Raynes Park to Chessington South
- ✧ Twickenham to Shepperton
- ✧ Twickenham to New Malden
- ✧ Lewisham to Hayes
- ✧ Euston to Watford local line

The following list was more adventurous, advocating extensions to parts of existing rail lines proposed for conversion to light rail, with streets being used for the extension, or to connect up adjacent rail lines. Exact details of proposed street alignments were not stated in the report, but obvious assumptions can be drawn as being the logical shortest and most appropriate street route to the quoted extension objective:

1 **Greenford to West Ruislip** over the Central Line with possible extension to Ruislip to connect with Uxbridge to Harrow section of the Metropolitan Line, also converted to light rail. Street running may have been required between West Ruislip and Ruislip.

2 **Watford Junction to Rickmansworth** light rail link replacing part of Metropolitan line and Croxley Green BR branch, with possible extension to St Albans.

3 **Finchley Central to High Barnet and Mill Hill East** replacing part of the Northern Line, with light rail beyond Mill Hill East to Edgware partially over abandoned line via Mill Hill The Hale.

4 **Chingford to Clapton** via BR line, then on street to Dalston Junction and Liverpool Street, or to Tottenham.

5 **Greenford to West Ealing line**, with diversion to streets in West Ealing, using the Uxbridge Road to reach Ealing Broadway.

6 **Elmers End to Addiscombe**, with street extension to East and West Croydon

7 **Purley to Tattenham Corner** via BR branch, then on street to Epsom Downs, then taking over Epsom Downs to Sutton BR branch.

8 **Slough to Windsor** via BR, new park and ride facility near M4, then on streets, using battery power to join SR Windsor Riverside to Staines line, extending to absorb Addlestone BR loop to Weybridge.

Another group of suggestions looked at completely new lines, some using abandoned rail corridors, whilst others were pure street or alongside street tramway proposals:

1 **Highgate to Wood Green** via former BR line to Alexandra Palace, then over private land, and along streets to Wood Green Station. (An adaptation of the proposal examined in the 1980 review.)

2 **South Bank Line**: Mainly street route also using riverside walks from Battersea to Surrey Docks via Waterloo and London Bridge. The report comments that *light railway subways or bridges might have to be constructed at major junctions*, and recommends that *battery power should be considered in sensitive areas*.

3 **Croydon to New Addington**: Still on the cards from earlier automatic minitram aspirations of the 1970s, but now seen as a conventional modern tramway

4 **Woolwich Arsenal to Thamesmead**. This was floated as a *new segregated and street running line, possibly linked to extension of the Docklands Light Railway. It would 'share or adjoin BR tracks where possible to avoid major road works at Plumstead.'*

5   **Cricklewood to Paddington/Marble Arch via Edgware Road**, then
    splitting to continue to Victoria and Oxford Circus. Effectively a straight bus
    to street tram conversion of the core of bus route 16. (This was one of the
    corridors suggested by Runnacles in 1977)

6   **Croydon to Brixton**: again a straight bus to tram proposal for the core part
    of bus route 109 (picking up on what had been looked at in 1979 as a
    minitram idea).

7   **Forest Hill to Elephant & Castle**: a bus to tram conversion over route
    171. (Mainly reviving a corridor suggested by Runnacles in 1977)

8   **Uxbridge Road**: bus to tram conversion of the entire 207 route (again, 1977
    revisited)

Four schemes were selected for closer examination in addition to possible extensions to the DLR. These were:

1   Conversion of the East London Line to light rail and extension into Liverpool
    Street.

2   A comprehensive study of the possible role of light rail in Croydon

3   A light rail link from Rickmansworth to Watford.

4   Conversion of part of the eastern end (Woodford to Hainault and Ongar) or
    western end (Northolt to West Ruislip) of the Central Line to light rail.

Of the above, Nos 1 and 4 fell by the wayside, whilst No.3 gave rise to the
Croxley heavy-rail link study. It is No 2 which of course is the basis of Tramlink.
The Croydon scheme was also considered attractive because it had the potential to form the nucleus of a light rail network. The map from the report used
to highlight possibilities in South London is reproduced overleaf. It shows
some of the more ambitious aims (LRV conversion of the Epsom Downs and
Tattenham Corner lines with 'lines along the edge of Epsom Downs' linking the
two termini, and direct conversion to light rail operation for the Caterham,
Hayes and Wimbledon via Sutton lines).

DEVELOPMENT OF TRAMLINK

Shortly after midday on 10th May 2000, tram 2550 became the first London
tram to operate in public service since 1952, when it ran from East Croydon
to New Addington. Subsequent route openings on 23rd May to Beckenham
Junction and on 30th May between Wimbledon and Elmers End completed the
Croydon Tramlink system as in service today.

   This was the culmination of nearly twelve years work behind the scenes and
three years construction work. The real start of the idea for the Tramlink system can probably be ascribed to a study carried out jointly by London Transport
and British Rail in 1986 entitled *Light Rail for London?*. This scrutinised 40
possible opportunities for conversion of existing or disused rail lines to light rail
operation as a way of increasing passenger usage and providing improved links.
As well as construction of a line from Croydon to New Addington, this featured
the idea of connecting existing/former secondary rail routes across Croydon town
centre by a street running line linking West and East Croydon.

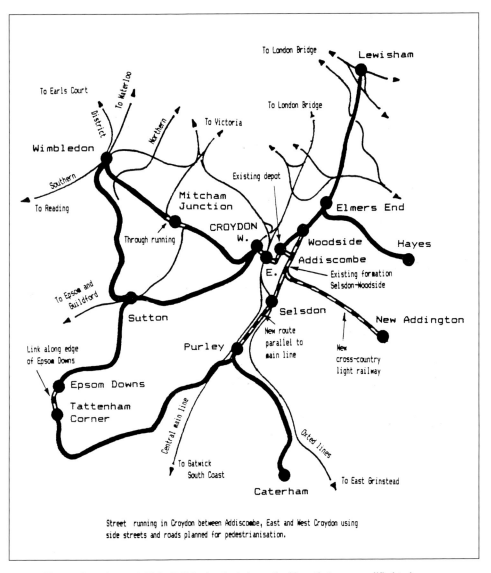

To London Bridge

Lewisham

To Earls Court

To Waterloo

District

Northern

To Victoria

To London Bridge

Wimbledon

Southern

Existing depot

Mitcham
Junction

Elmers End

To Reading

CROYDON
W.

Woodside

Hayes

Through running

Addiscombe

E.

Existing formation
Selsdon-Woodside

To Epsom and
Guildford

Sutton

Selsdon

New Addington

Purley

New route
parallel to
main line

New
cross-country
light railway

Link along edge
of Epsom Downs

Epsom Downs

Central main line

Tattenham
Corner

Oxted lines

To Gatwick
South Coast

To East Grinstead

Caterham

Street running in Croydon between Addiscombe, East and West Croydon using
side streets and roads planned for pedestrianisation.

This map from the 1986 'Light Rail for London' shows the ideas that were modified to become
Tramlink. Wimbledon to West Croydon is there, with the comment 'through running' shown at
Mitcham Junction, envisaging track sharing there rather than total separation. The street link
across Croydon, and the new 'cross country' railway to Addington are there, whereas light rail
use of the former Selsdon line south of Blackhorse Lane is not only planned as far as Coombe
Road, but also provides a passage over its southern alignment to enable light rail to link into
the Caterham and Tattenham Corner plans. Perhaps most curious was a comment above the
map which suggested that DC conductor rail might continue, with overhead or battery power
being used on some extensions.

A detailed study was commissioned in 1987, with the participation of the London Borough of Croydon. Its recommendations were that an initial network of three lines radiating from central Croydon to Wimbledon, Elmers End and New Addington would be technically and economically feasible and worthy of further investigation. Further detailed studies ensued and in June 1990 a final study was awarded to a consortium of consultants to carry out a detailed definition of a light rail scheme, an assessment of its environmental, economic and financial feasibility with a view to full public consultation on route options. The report from this study became the basis of the scheme jointly promoted by LT and the Borough, leading to the Croydon Tramlink Parliamentary Bill deposited in 1991.

The Department of Transport insisted that the private sector should also be involved in the development of the project and private sector partners were chosen to join LT and London Borough of Croydon in a Project Development Group whose main tasks were to develop a system specification, financial forecasts and concession arrangements.

The Croydon Tramlink Bill was deposited in 1991 as a private member's procedure. The third reading in the Commons took place in July 1994 and Royal Assent was granted on 21st July 1994. Tramlink was the last transport project under the Parliamentary Bill procedure and subsequent schemes came under the Transport and Works Act 1992 procedure.

Mock-up of Sheffield-type car displayed outside Croydon Town Hall, March 1991.

In December 1994, public funding for the Croydon Tramlink and Midlands Metro projects was agreed under the government's Private Finance Initiative. A competition to finance, develop, build, operate and maintain the complete system was launched by Steven Norris, MP on 30th May 1995. The pre-qualification competition produced eight applications, which were then slimmed down to four groups. Bids had to be submitted in January 1996 and in April 1996 Tramtrack Croydon Ltd. (TCL) was announced as the preferred bidder.

TCL is a consortium consisting of:

CentreWest Ltd (now part of FirstGroup) – the operator
Bombardier Transportation – tram suppliers and maintainers
Royal Bank of Scotland – project finance
3i – project finance
Sir Robert McAlpine – forming the Construction
Amey Construction plc – Joint Venture (CJV)

In order to reduce the cost of the scheme to a level acceptable to the government various cost saving schemes were agreed. On 25th November 1996 a 99-year concession was awarded to TCL, with a predicted opening date of 4th November 1999. The government agreed a grant of £125 million towards the scheme, which included a substantial amount for LT to pay for all the statutory undertakers' works necessary before actual tramway construction could begin.

CONSTRUCTION AND EQUIPMENT

To undertake the construction programme, the two civil engineering members of the Tramtrack consortium, Sir Robert McAlpine and Amey Construction, formed a Construction Joint Venture (CJV). Utilities diversions started on 6th January 1997 and were substantially complete by August 1998; these works were undertaken directly for London Transport. Following delivery of the first tram in September 1998, dynamic testing and commissioning commenced. Proving of vehicles and systems was initially over a test section of track between Beddington Lane and Ampere Way, subsequently extending over the rest of the system by late July 1999. Test running on the Wimbledon line was completed in October 1999, but full commissioning of the town centre section was delayed by technical problems and it was not possible to undertake full-scale trial running until early in 2000. Confidence in operation of the system was rapidly gained so that opening could be fixed for May 2000.

Tracklaying in progress at Lodge Lane, New Addington.

INFRASTRUCTURE DESIGN

The section through South Norwood Country Park on the Beckenham line is new construction as is the New Addington branch from Larcombe Close to New Addington terminus and on these sections some major earthworks were required. The whole system impacted on over 80 existing structures, all of which had to be assessed and, where necessary, modified for Tramlink operation.

Tramlink utilises former railway corridors for almost half of its length, and these had to be fully separated from Railtrack infrastructure. This included grade separation at two locations. Mitcham Junction flyover is a single span steel plate girder crossing the Railtrack lines to Hackbridge. It uses pre-cast concrete units to form the deck rather than steel troughing and sits on re-inforced concrete bank seats which in turn rest on reinforced soil approach embankments. Wandle Park viaduct was a difficult structure to design and build as it was on a site constrained by a road, a public park, the railway to West Croydon, and the existing railway corridor which Tramlink took over, with awkward horizontal and vertical alignments. The solution was the use of pre-cast pre-stressed Y beams for the span across the railway with in-situ construction in conventional reinforced concrete for the side spans, the total length containing five spans with two curves over its length.

The existing bridge at East Croydon Station over the railway was found to consist of many separate elements, some of which were found to be unsuitable for carrying Tramlink loading. One span was replaced with pre-cast concrete beams whilst another was updated by removing the old trough infill and replacing with lightweight concrete. Five other existing bridges were also re-decked for Tramlink use.

TRACKWORK

Existing trackwork was of a variety of forms and in a range of conditions and 8km of this was refurbished and reused on the main line, with a further 1km reused in the stabling at the depot. Off street the new track supplied generally consists of S49 section flat-bottom rail secured with Vossloh pattern clips to pre-stressed concrete Monobloc sleepers on track ballast. For the street sections a reinforced concrete track slab was utilised with embedded rails. Grooved rail of either type Ri59 or Ri60 is embedded into slots saw-cut into the concrete track slab. It is secured in cold-curing polymer, which provides electrical and vibration insulation from the track slab, and holds the rail to gauge.

Pointwork was supplied by Voest-Alpine (VAE) of Austria and is equipped with operating mechanisms by Hanning and Kahl. Although there are, excluding the depot, 48 sets of points on the system, only nine sets, where route selection is required are motorised, and all other points are sprung as movement is always in the trailing direction. The motorised points at junctions are set by local equipment which communicates with an approaching tram and reacts to the destination code which has been preset on the transponder fitted underneath the tram. Emergency crossovers are manually set by tram drivers using point levers. Indicators are provided at all points normally used in the facing direction to advise the tram drivers that the route is correctly set.

In total there are just under 52 track kilometres making up the 28km system. The Wimbledon and Beckenham lines are a mixture of double track and single track. Croydon town centre consists of a single track one-way 'loop'. The New Addington line is all double track with the exception of a short length near the terminus at New Addington. Track speeds range from 80kph in the rural sections to as little as 15kph in the town.

POWER SUPPLY SYSTEM

The system operates at a nominal 750V dc with a peak power consumption of 1MW in any section. To provide power to the system 13 substations were built. The masts are generally galvanised steel column H-section although a few in the conservation area in the centre of Croydon are circular hollow sections. Also in the town centre, the use of 22 masts, mostly in George Street, was avoided by use of fixings on sufficiently strong buildings, with span wires. Bracket arms are cantilevered to carry the contact wires from the masts with stay rods attached to them. Registration is controlled using steady arms. The wire is hung from the masts using Kevlar cables which also provide electrical isolation. The contact wire consists of two 107mm^2 grooved section copper wires of inverted omega section, but a single wire is sufficient in the depot area where current draw is lower.

CONTROL AND COMMUNICATIONS

The system operates on a line of sight basis. However, there are places on the system where signals are required, such as road crossings, junctions and single line sections. For the latter, an automatic system is provided so that once a tram has entered a single line section from one direction, a stop signal is displayed at the loop at the other end of the section. There is also an emergency back-up alarm system.

To operate the system efficiently, tram detection is provided so that the controllers know where each vehicle is in the system. The position of each tram, along with details of its schedule, are displayed on a graphic screen in the control room. The 13 substations are remotely monitored by the controllers at the depot using a Supervisory Control And Data Acquisition (SCADA) system. Through SCADA the controllers can, if necessary, isolate sections of the overhead line by switching off the power at the substations.

In the control room the various subsystems are displayed on monitors using the Control Centre Integrated Computer System. This consists of three workstations which, using menu screens, can be used to examine or control any of the sub-systems above. Should there be an alarm anywhere on the system these are immediately brought to the attention of the controllers.

TRAMSTOPS

On street sections, stops are mostly raised footways whilst off street they are similar to railway stations. Most stops have shelters with seating, a ticket machine, a passenger information point, CCTV camera, a help point and lighting. The stops are designed for disabled use with the front edge very close to the threshold of the tram door so that wheelchair users can access the vehicle unaided. Tactile paving and colour contrasts are used to aid the visually impaired. Ramps are provided to access the stops from roads or footpaths.

TICKET VENDING MACHINES

Tramlink is operated on an open boarding basis and there is no ticket check as a passenger boards the tram. Passengers without a pre-purchased Travelcard or concessionary pass must purchase one from a ticket vending machine at the tram stop. The system is backed up by frequent ticket checks and a high penalty fare.

The ticket machines are robust units derived from models already successfully deployed on similar systems in Europe. Supplied by Schlumberger, the machines accept a variety of notes as well as the usual coins and dispense change. As with all of the system the machines have also been designed for use by the disabled. Ticket selection is made using a menu driven screen and a selector wheel/button.

DEPOT

The depot is situated at Therapia Lane on the Wimbledon branch. The depot building provides four maintenance bays with associated equipment including hoists, an overhead crane, a wheel lathe and synchronised jacks for lifting a complete tram. In addition on the ground floor there are changing rooms and maintenance offices. Main offices are on the first floor, including the control room. Outside there are facilities to replenish the sand hoppers on the trams and to wash them. At the western side of the complex are the stabling sidings where all 24 vehicles are kept overnight.

There is sufficient space to extend the sidings for more trams if necessary in the future.

THE TRAMS

The Tramtrack Croydon Ltd consortium's vehicle manufacturing member was Bombardier Transportation. The design was based on the K4000 articulated tram supplied to Cologne, Germany, but lengthened by about 1.5m.

The tram has two almost 'mirror-image' sections connected by a short central section over a central bogie, with articulations between each part. Overall length is 30.1 metres and width 2.65 metres, with each end slightly tapered. The low floor area of 400 mm height, with an entrance height of 350mm from the top of the rail, extends over 76% of the passenger compartment. There is a single step up from this area to a higher floor section over the power bogie at each end, each containing 16 seats. In total there are 70 seats in the vehicle and a further 138 standing passengers can be accommodated at a spacing of 4 passengers per square metre. A position for one wheelchair is sited between the first two sets of offside doors in each section. On each side of the tram are four 1305mm wide doorways with sliding plug type doors. Doorways are symmetrical on each side. Internally, the trams are finished in a light grey colour scheme, with blue seat covers and yellow high visibility stanchions and handrails.

The driver's cabs have exterior inward-opening doors to the offside and also have an opening door into the saloon. The driver's seat is sited slightly to the nearside.

A tram on the New Addington route passes through Lloyd Park.

The electrical equipment and running gear is supplied by Kiepe Elektrik of Düsseldorf in Germany. Four 120kW 3-phase asynchronous motors are fitted to the two powered two-axle bogies towards the ends of the tram and there is an unpowered independent four-wheel bogie under the central articulation. Bogies have rubber/metal primary suspension with coil spring secondary suspension. Sanders are fitted to each of the eight powered wheels. An anti-slip and slide system is provided.

Three different brake systems are fitted: an electric regenerative service brake, an hydraulic/mechanical disc brake and a magnetic track brake.

Current at 750V dc is collected from the overhead by a Shunk type pantograph fitted above the inner pair of doors on one section of the tram. Low voltage equipment on the tram is at 24V dc.

The tram is capable of a maximum speed of 80kmph (50 mph) and can accelerate at up to $1.2m/s^2$. Normal braking rate at 80kmph is 1.3m/s2 although in an emergency this is $2.75m/s^2$.

The trams are numbered in a sequence from 2530 to 2553. These numbers follow on directly from the highest numbered previous London tram.

The first tram was completed in Vienna by June 1998 and then underwent exhaustive testing at the BWS plant and on a test track in Vienna, ready for trial operation following arrival in the UK on 15th September 1998. The remaining 23 trams were delivered in sequence between September 1998 and June 1999.

TRAMLINK'S ROUTES

Fanning out from Croydon town centre, Tramlink runs to four separate terminals, three on the east side of Croydon and one to the west. All four sections make some use of previous rail alignments.

From the west, the Wimbledon – Croydon line mostly follows the former railway line between the towns and joins the rest of the system at Reeves Corner junction, on the town centre one-way loop. This loop follows various streets, mostly too narrow for double track, to George Street where a reserved double track section continues past East Croydon Station. East of here, the first section along Addiscombe Road consists of double track in a residential road moving to a side reservation on the south side of Addiscombe Road. At Sandilands trams descend to the former Woodside – Selsdon rail alignment and turn sharp left for the Beckenham and Elmers End routes or right for New Addington. The New Addington route is mostly a new reserved track tramway with steep gradients through woodland and open country, roadside running as well as tunnels on the old rail alignment. The Beckenham/Elmers End line follows former rail corridors except for the new section from Arena through South Norwood Country Park to Birkbeck. The short Elmers End line diverges from the Beckenham route at Arena junction.

TRAMLINK SERVICES

Route 1 provides a cross-Croydon service from Wimbledon to Elmers End, only westbound trams serving George Street and Church Street stops whilst eastbound trams observe West Croydon and Wellesley Road stops. The daytime service is every 10 minutes. The other two routes follow the one-way loop round the town centre to give excellent penetration and provide a through service to and from West Croydon. Route 2 runs between Beckenham Junction and the central Croydon loop every 10 minutes daytime and route 3 runs between New Addington and Central Croydon every 5–7 minutes daytime.

In evenings and on Sundays the basic frequency is 30 minutes on routes 1 and 2, and 15 minutes on route 3. However, to give a better service through to Wimbledon, route 2 is extended from central Croydon to Wimbledon during these periods. The normal daytime timetable requires eight trams in service on route 1, five on route 2 and eight on route 3, a total of 21 out of the fleet of 24. The full service runs during Monday to Friday peak hours, between the peak hours and during Saturday shopping hours.

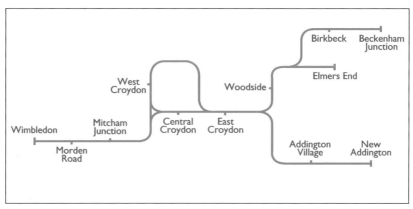

TRAMLINK EXTENSION PROPOSALS

Ridership of Tramlink reached over 16,000,000 per year after the first year of operation of the existing system. Passenger demand continues to rise and local authorities and residents are keen to see the Tramlink extended to other areas.

An initial review of potential Tramlink extensions has been prepared and discussed with interested parties. T/L now wishes to carry out initial development and evaluation work on possible routes to Sutton, Tooting, Mitcham, Purley, Coulsdon, Streatham and Crystal Palace. Furthermore, there will be a need to give preliminary examination to other extension proposals. These include suggestions to connect Tramlink to Lewisham, Bromley town centre, Biggin Hill Airport/Village and examining a local spur/loop to penetrate further into Purley Way retail/industrial park.

Starting in the west, there are two corridors that suggest bringing Tramlink to Sutton town centre. The first of these, proposing operations principally between Wimbledon and Sutton has been in view even before Tramlink opened. Indeed, presumptuously, the trams were delivered with destination displays for this as 'line 4' already included on blind sets.

SUTTON – WIMBLEDON

This proposal utilises the existing Tramlink infrastructure between Wimbledon and Morden Road stop. The cramped tram terminus inside Wimbledon station is barely adequate for its present function. If another service is to arrive at Wimbledon a new terminus will need to be created. Diverging from the present Croydon route the Sutton line might adopt segregated alignment within the highway along Morden Road, serving Morden station interchange. It would probably use Aberconway Road to reach Morden Hall Road before using the spacious St Helier Avenue as the direct route to St Helier, Rose Hill. St Helier Hospital is an important local traffic objective that Tramlink ought to serve, despite the need to deviate from the direct route into Sutton via Angel Hill. A number of variants in Sutton town centre are to be examined to see how the shopping centre, station and office complex can be accessed. The alignment is presently served by a number of busy bus services and if built, would give Tramlink patrons direct interchange with the Northern Line at Morden. A south to east curve may also be considered at Morden Road to permit direct operations that link St Helier to Mitcham and Croydon.

SUTTON – TOOTING AND MITCHAM JUNCTION – MITCHAM

The other Sutton proposal – to Tooting – is more ambitious and undoubtedly contains many more challenges than a Sutton/Wimbledon link. Apart from workshop/depot facilities and a curve required to link the line into the existing system, this extension would share no infrastructure with the existing Tramlink. Were 'line 4' to be realised ahead of this proposal, the Tooting line would of course then have the St Helier to Sutton section in common. North of St Helier, the alignment is likely to fit across parkland and open space to take in the Willow Lane Industrial Estate before serving Mitcham town centre. Some commonality would be enjoyed here with the short separate proposal to provide a spur from Mitcham Junction to Mitcham town centre. From here, the Tooting projection would seek to use the pedestrianised town centre section before sharing carriageway with all traffic in the part of London Road south of Figge's Marsh, with room for segregation beyond the junction with Streatham Road. The most difficult leg arises immediately the Merton/Wandsworth boundary is crossed and the most effective way of reaching Tooting Broadway from this point will stir much debate.

NORTH AND SOUTH FROM CROYDON

These are currently extremely busy bus corridors. Not surprisingly, the first generation trams were the mainstay on the Purley – Croydon – Streatham section and former tram lines 16 and 18, once amongst the most successful in London, ran beyond here to Brixton and central London. In this exercise, the corridor is to be reviewed as two separate extensions.

The proposal envisages Tramlink diverging from its central Croydon loop to pick up highway alignment probably using South End, and Brighton Road to Purley. Investigations will reveal whether the mass passenger movement achieved today by buses is more effectively catered for by a Tramlink extension. Beyond Purley, work will look at Coulsdon as a southern terminus within striking distance of the end of the M23. An important consideration here will be the possibility of a Park and Ride site that might funnel current car traffic into Croydon from the south onto public transport. Alignment difficulties will be more critical south of Purley, where Brighton Road carries the A23 trunk road traffic.

North of Croydon, London Road is again the obvious host for a Tramlink extension. South of Thornton Heath Pond, the shared carriageway is a possibility. North of this point, the road becomes the A23 again, but fortunately there are likely to be some opportunities for tram segregation to Norbury and between Norbury and Streatham, although Norbury itself is a pinch point. Streatham Station will increase in importance as in interchange with the East London Line extension and this is envisaged as the northern terminus of the Tramlink extension. Whilst there is considerable merit in looking beyond Streatham, the challenge of the Streatham Library pinchpoint is perhaps one for a later date.

CRYSTAL PALACE

The nature of this proposal is vastly different from the others under review. In essence it looks to replace a local low-frequency conventional rail service with a more attractive tram service between Beckenham Junction and Crystal Palace Station. If this is achieved, it makes sense to incorporate a west to south curve at Love Lane so that a Crystal Palace to Croydon service could be provided.

For a number of reasons, track sharing with heavy rail is not an option. Therefore even if heavy rail were to be removed east of the Norwood Junction North flyover, a Tramlink extension would need to adopt a new alignment to immediately north of this point, since other rail services utilise the track here on the more frequent services between London and Crystal Palace and on through Norwood Junction. Work in hand will explore the possibilities, but the more obvious course is to aim for Anerley Road which passes the street entrance to Crystal Palace Station. The steeply graded peak of Anerley Hill presents another severe challenge on the direct route to reach the logical transport interchange at Crystal Palace Parade. Alternative alignments that may need to encroach on part of Crystal Palace Park are likely to be unacceptable.

As a by-product of this extension, the operational environment over the Beckenham leg of the existing system would be considerably improved since the main part of the currently shared corridor between Beckenham Junction and Beckenham Cemetery could be occupied instead by a double tramway track.

KINGSTON LIGHT RAIL
PROPOSALS 1990

Fulwell
Somerset Road
Hampton Hill
Teddington
Kempton Park
Bushy Park Road
Sunbury
Hampton Wick
P&R
Hampton
Kingston
Upper Halliford
Clarence Street
Fairfield
(alternatives)
Villiers Road
Shepperton
Surbiton
Berrylands
Crescent
Malden Way
Surbiton
Malden Manor
Tolworth
Chessington North
Chessington South
Malden Rushett
P&R
Epsom Hospital
Epsom

- - - - - British Rail alignment
——— Partially segregated alignment
.... Street running alignment
P&R Park & Ride

Drawn by Mike Harris

KINGSTON LIGHT RAIL STUDY

Croydon was not the only scheme to warrant further attention after the 1986 *Light Rail For London?* report. This had identified two existing rail routes in the Kingston area which might benefit from conversion to light rail. One was the New Malden to Twickenham section of the Kingston loop, along with the Shepperton branch, whilst the other was the Chessington branch.

Fired by the idea, the Royal Borough of Kingston upon Thames, Surrey County Council and London Transport carried out further investigations, amending and expanding their aspirations before eventually the consulting engineers Ove Arup & Partners were commissioned for a Kingston Light Rail Study. This report, issued in stages late in 1990 and early 1991, examined three possible routes. The first was the Kingston to Shepperton option, taking over from BR. It concluded that this should not be pursued, on the grounds that the route would not cover operating costs, and would present disbenefits for through travellers. The other two options were examined in greater depth, and proposals were as follows:

1   Kingston town centre to Epsom via the Hogsmill Valley, part of the Chessington rail branch, and on to Epsom station via Epsom hospitals.
2   Kingston town centre to Surbiton station.

Detailed plans for both routes were drawn up, a depot location proposed at Kingsmead, and proposals for crossing major obstacles, such as the A3 trunk road, studied in depth. The Surbiton line was planned to be street running throughout, using a combination of single and double track as appropriate. From a Surbiton station terminus planned for the station forecourt and encroaching onto part of the station car park, two options were looked at: One was via Victoria Road, Brighton Road, Portsmouth Road, High Street and Eden Street, whilst the version taken forward for more detailed study ran via Claremont Road, Surbiton Crescent, Surbiton Road, Penrhyn Road, Wheatfield Way, Brook Street and Eden Street. In the centre of Kingston, the route was planned via Clarence Street, London Road, Caversham Road, Fairfield Road, returning via Fairfield Road, Wheatfield Way, Clarence Street and on to Eden Street. An alternative deviated to use an anti-clockwise loop Via Clarence Street, Wood Street, Clarence Street. Another option was a terminal stub at the southern end of Castle Street.

The Epsom route would leave the loop to swing into London Road, no doubt causing relocation of the famous statuesque K6 telephone boxes on the way. Minerva Road would see the line turn southwards, continuing down Villiers Road before leaving the streets to run on low embankment between Athelstan Recreation Ground and the Hogsmill River. Just before crossing the river, a depot site was earmarked at Kingsmead. Continuing on segregated right of way, cutting under the main Waterloo to Portsmouth railway line close to Berrylands, it would then run on viaduct over the A3, and eventually join the existing Chessington BR branch. From this point, the light rail would adopt the northernmost track to run alongside the continuing but single tracked heavy rail to Chessington South. Beyond that point, the line would adopt part of the railway cutting to reach a point near Chessington Zoo, or 'World of Adventures' in today's parlance. Interestingly, civil works were in place for a planned extension of the BR line to serve Malden Rushett and Leatherhead North before joining the line from Epsom to Leatherhead, but the railway extension was stillborn. After the Zoo, the light rail line would have gone eastwards across farmland and then take an undetermined course through the site of the former Epsom Hospitals area, proposed for housing development. Street running would be resumed at the junction of West Hill with Stamford Green Road, rising to terminate alongside Epsom BR station.

The study envisaged modern tramways employing low floor cars, with plans and calculations drawn up accordingly, and the report predicted that both lines would be viable in terms of operating revenue over costs, and in reducing the private car traffic entering the centre of Kingston. The construction and set up capital costs at 1990 prices were estimated to be in the region of £84m. There the case rested until 1994 when the Borough, still hankering after light rail and seeing the Croydon Tramlink scheme progressing towards reality, blew the dust off the earlier study. This time, the plans were expanded beyond the original scheme to take on board both Surbiton alignments and a vintage line, based on the success of this type of operation in the USA, to link Kingston with Hampton Court. Despite renewed local enthusiasm, the prospects for the return of trams to Kingston looked bleak at the time of writing (2001), with greater potential elsewhere stealing the limelight.

BARKING TOWN TRAMWAY

In 1991, the London Borough of Barking & Dagenham approached London Transport about possible forms of transport which could integrate developments in the River Roding/Town Quay area into the existing Barking shopping area and station. Initial ideas centred on a possible heritage tramway which would add to the tourist and leisure attractions of the borough as well as providing the new transport link. Heritage tramways under the banner *Vintage Trolley* had taken off in a big way in the USA, with the dual function of tourist attraction combined with functional transport facility. Things had been slower elsewhere, although Stockholm's line 7 was reintroduced as a vintage line as a prelude to further light rail development, and in the early 1990s the first new British *Vintage* line was being planned in Birkenhead. Vintage operation can provide a safe and basic light rail facility which can bring considerable cost savings in construction and operation when compared to the state of the art technology that modern light rail can offer, so long as the expectations are less ambitious. The Borough had also consulted Ove Arup & Partners on the same theme.

London Transport's report of January 1992 examined the scheme in detail. Maps within the document showed the line using part of the pedestrianised East Street before shooting off west across parkland and over a new bridge across the Roding to reach the new development site on the west bank of the river. Variants used London Road/North Street or Clockhouse Avenue, although a more ambitious option suggested a one way frying pan, out via London Road to the A406 roundabout, then south alongside the east bank of the Roding, which it crossed to reach the development site. Return would be as per the first idea, thus requiring two new bridges across the river. The report indicated possible construction costs of a vintage line with basic trackworks in the range of £2 to £4m.

Other extensions were discussed in the report, including eastwards via Longbridge Road to Barking bus garage, or westwards to serve developments proposed for Gallions Reach and to interchange with the DLR Beckton extension. The link to Docklands was amplified later in the report, and referred to a 1989 study which envisaged the extension of the DLR from Beckton to Barking that had been rejected on cost grounds. To compensate for this, the Barking Town Tram report looked at proposals to project beyond the River Roding site to Jenkins Lane, under the A13, and then via Windsor Estate to reach Beckton DLR, or to Gallions Reach DLR.

The 1992 report collected dust after its production, until a revised approach was received from Barking & Dagenham Council in late 1993. Another proposed development at Barking Reach, which gained only a cursory mention in the 1992 report, was the main feature of this approach, and London Transport carried out study work culminating in a report to the council in 1993 discussing options for serving Barking Reach.

On 23/24 June 1994, coinciding with a Light Rail conference in Barking Town Hall, articles of light rail and modern bus technology were on public display around the bandstand and in the pedestrianised precinct in East Street, Barking. A short length of portable narrow gauge track was laid along part of East Street and demonstration rides were provided by flywheel driven Parry Peoplemover cars. The then Minister for Transport in London, Steven Norris, addressed the conference, and inspected the display.

A publicity leaflet was distributed suggesting a light rail line from Barking Station to Barking Reach. The map on the leaflet indicated an alignment via Ripple Road, King Edwards Road, Perth Road, Greatfields Park, Movers Lane, Bastable Avenue, and then south through an industrial estate into land earmarked for the Barking Reach housing development. This scheme was clearly not on the basis of a vintage line, although the viability forecasts increased if costs could be trimmed by going for basic rather than *state of the art* equipment.

Further discussion took place between the Council, property developers and London Transport into 1994 and 1995, although the proposal was to be mode non-specific for the time being, with guided bus possibilities to be considered as an alternative option. One reason for the slow progress was that the development at Barking Reach would not grow as quickly as earlier indications had suggested. It would have been sheer folly to invest the full cost of light rail infrastructure at an early stage to cater for a slowly growing development which might not be complete for 10 or more years.

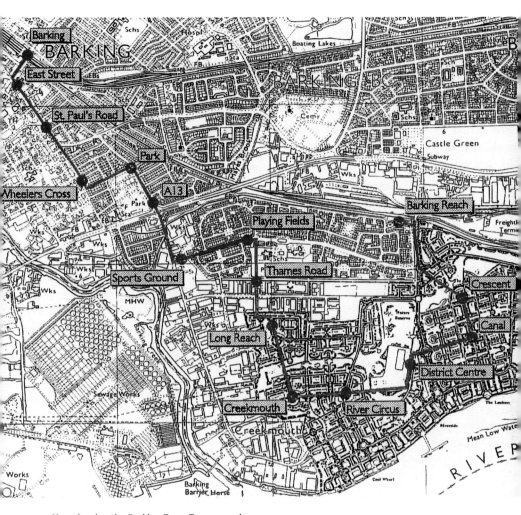

Map showing the Barking Town Tramway scheme.

Further to this, the Barking Reach scheme was close to a wider *Thames Gateway* regeneration and transport study. Other schemes for transport development involving adjacent boroughs were on the cards, and some of these were also looking at guided bus as a solution. Barking became further and further embedded into the wider East Thames plans and its future as a light rail possibility faded as the East London Transit proposals for bus or trolleybus based solutions gathered strength towards initial public consultation in July 2001.

GREENWICH WATERFRONT TRANSIT

On 5th January 1995, An article entitled 'Riverfront trams system plans are on the right track – town bosses reveal rail good idea.' appeared in the *South London Mercury*. This revealed proposals for a modern tramway to link Greenwich, Charlton, Woolwich and Thamesmead with the Jubilee Line extension station at North Greenwich. This followed an approach by Greenwich Council to London Transport during the previous October exploring the possibilities of a rapid transit link to the Greenwich Peninsula, site of the new tube station. There were also plans for a Millennium festival on the Greenwich Peninsula, and the Council were keen to move as quickly as possible in an attempt to have the line in place in time for both of these events. In the longer term, the Council viewed the tramway as an attractive alternative to private car traffic movements in and around Greenwich and Woolwich town centres. It was also intending to widen Woolwich Road, part of which was to accommodate a street running tramway. A further announcement about the Greenwich scheme appeared in *LT News* on 23rd February 1995 quoting an estimated set-up cost of £60m.

Given the short timescale, LT agreed to help, and an initial report recommended that a tramway be constructed from North Greenwich via new roads around the station and part of an old rail freight alignment, Bugsbys Way, Anchor & Hope Lane, Woolwich Road and into the Woolwich Arsenal development. Further extensions would follow to Thamesmead in the east, and a spur to Greenwich station to the south west. In 1995, Greenwich Council were very keen to drive this scheme in time for the opening of North Greenwich station and the peninsula Millennium Festival, although later recommendations by LT and TfL offered buses or trolleybuses as possible alternatives to trams for this scheme. The proposals eventually developed into Greenwich Waterfront Transit, on which the initial public consultation exercise was carried out during July 2001.

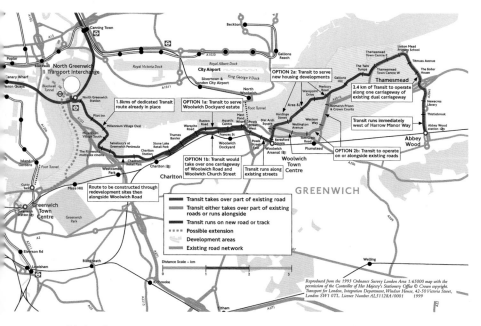

THE SILVERTOWN TRAMWAY

On 15th February 1995, the *Financial Times* suggested that London's Docklands could have a tram system to complement the DLR. It revealed LDDC/LT plans for a £14m proposal to connect new developments in the Silvertown area with existing transport nodes. The line would link Canning Town via King George V Dock and new streets in Silvertown to North Woolwich. The newspaper quaintly reported that the new line would use 'buses modified for rail use' and some disused rail track (part of the original Silvertown Tramway alignment). In discussing the power supply, it spoke of a choice between conventional over-head wires and what is actually the Parry Peoplemover system where an underfloor flywheel system re-energised at stops from an external power source drives the tram.

An earlier report in *Docklands News* was more accurate and more compre-hensive. It talked of a £12m tramway to run from Canning Town to North Woolwich which 'could be ready in time for the opening of the Jubilee Line Extension in 1998'. This report considered trams, costing less than £100,000 each rather than the more usual £1.5+, which could carry 25 seated passengers plus the same number standing. Unusually, metre gauge tracks were proposed, which would have inhibited integration if any standard gauge tramways ever approached the Royal Docks area. The option to use overhead or 'roadside con-tacts' was a correct interpretation of the yet to be decided power system – i.e. conventional or flywheel Parry Peoplemover System. The scheme was to be developed by Newham Council, the LDDC and London Transport, and the report hinted at a franchise of 25 years being offered.

A phased construction programme was suggested, with the first being from Silvertown Urban Village to St Marks Church and to Royal Victoria DLR station. Stage two would push the line through to Canning Town, whilst the ultimate extension would take over the existing North London line alignment into North Woolwich if plans for diversion of the heavy rail line to Woolwich were to mate-rialise. By the turn of the century, these proposals had been consigned to the fantasy graveyard.

TRAMS FOR CHISWICK?

According to press reports in March 1996, there was a groundswell of local opinion keen to push for a tramway from Kensington High Street through Hammersmith and Chiswick. Local MP Nirj Deva had approached the then Minister for Transport in London and received enthusiastic support. However, nothing further was developed, and this line, which would have re-created part of London's first electric tramway, has so far remained just an idea.

NEW IDEAS FOR PUBLIC TRANSPORT IN OUTER LONDON

In June 1995, LT's then Director Of Planning, David Bayliss oversaw the issue of a report entitled *New Ideas for Public Transport in Outer London*. This document was primarily aimed at local councils and 'movers and shakers' in industry. It outlined the range of what were grouped together as 'intermediate modes' and spelt out their capabilities, comparative costs and effectiveness, and claimed to be a study based on the outer London boroughs only on the basis that a greater challenge existed to attract people to public transport there than in inner London, although it promised a future similar review for the areas left out of this report. This uncomfortable term 'intermediate modes' was defined as 'public transport modes with costs and capacities lying between heavy rail and conventional bus'. Along with tramways/light rail, this definition extended to busways, trolleybuses and duobuses (trolleybuses with a diesel engine option).

In his introduction, David Bayliss referred to the 1986 *Light Rail for London?* report, and how this led eventually to the Croydon Tramlink scheme. He recognised that the time was now ripe to view the whole range of public transport solutions and to understand how and where each of these could encourage greater use of public transport. Clues behind the increasingly urgent and expanding remit came early in the report where a number of statements from governmental bodies were quoted. These hinted at the need to reduce reliance on the private car, encourage energy efficient modes of transport and tackle road congestion and air pollution.

A review of studies then currently in progress included mention of the heavy rail link between Woolwich and Silvertown (commonly referred to as the *Woolwich Metro*) designed to channel Kentish lines across the river to improve integration with north London lines and to relieve the pressure on south London termini. A series of local connections into it on both sides of the Thames were shown on an accompanying map of an area being marketed for regeneration under the *Thames Gateway* banner. Specific mention was made of the Barking Reach Light Rapid Transit option. Reference to other lines in the Thames Gateway area extended from Docklands along the river frontage to Grays on the north side and to Gravesend on the south side. Spurs branched off to Dagenham Heathway and Elm Park, and Abbey Wood, as well as loops to serve Ebbsfleet and Dartford. No mention was made to the specific mode. A line connecting Greenwich town centre, Woolwich and Thamesmead to North Greenwich LUL station also appeared on the map, reflecting the desires of Greenwich Council to see a Tramlink-style solution, but again without confirmation of transport mode. The review mentioned other schemes where study work was under way including Tramlink extensions to Sutton, Norbury/Purley, and Colliers Wood, the A23 corridor to Brixton and beyond, and the Kingston light rail proposals as well as other ideas not involving light rail such as guided bus proposals for Park Royal.

Following a description of different modes and their strengths and weaknesses a useful bar chart compared cost (split into capital and operating cost) per passenger for conventional bus with segregated busway, segregated trolleybus and light rail starting to compete favourably on annual total costs per passenger with conventional bus on corridors where 2000 passengers per hour require movement leaping into a very clear lead over all other modes at the 4000 per hour level.

A wide range of possible study areas was shown on a map of Greater London and brief details were given of each idea but this was shortlisted to nine cases singled out for in-depth study as a matter of urgency. Providing that the studies prove each case to be viable, a timetable indicated that each project will move to full project definition stage during 1996, with statutory processes progressing during the following year, leading to detailed design and construction targeted for the 1998 to 2000 period.

In the list of proposals, only those that sprung directly from the basic Croydon Tramlink scheme were initially labelled as tramways. As a deliberate point of policy, none of the other proposals was noted as mode specific so that various modes can be tested against each proposal to establish the most appropriate choice to match each individual case.

The nine proposals for each case study were listed alongside their stated objectives as follows:

NORTH GREENWICH/NORTH BEXLEY

'To provide local public transport links to key development sites of Thames Gateway inner areas; provide a high quality feeder service to the Jubilee Line and on to Greenwich; to assist in the development and regeneration of the Greenwich waterfront and revitalisation of Woolwich town centre; to provide feeders for proposed Woolwich Metro.' Early press reports provided a strong indication that a tramway/light rail solution was favoured.

CROYDON – STREATHAM – BRIXTON (A23 CORRIDOR)

'To improve the quality of public transport along the corridor; to assist in the generation of Brixton and Streatham town centres; to bring wider environmental benefits.' – Clearly, light rail could feature as a logical solution on such a busy corridor which would plug into Tramlink (and its Norbury proposal) at one end, and central London proposals (not dealt with in this report) at the other.

TRAMLINK EXTENSIONS

'To provide high quality public transport links in the boroughs of Merton and Sutton.' This basically formalised current examination of locally inspired ideas. They were considered as Tramlink extensions because the basic line would already be in place. The individual cost of providing a service which shares some existing infrastructure must be below the cost that would be incurred for an entirely new stand-alone line.

UXBRIDGE CORRIDOR AND THE GREENFORD TO WEST EALING LINE

'Existing heavily used bus corridor from Uxbridge to Shepherds Bush. Possible extensions further into central London and to Greenford via BR branch at West Ealing to improve public transport quality and hence ridership and market share; to assist in the regeneration of Southall and Acton town centres; to bring wider environmental benefits.'

The Uxbridge Road is well known for its long stretches of wide road or dual carriageway, and it was of course once home to the famous 'Feltham' tramcars on route 7. Whilst there is some possibility that these objectives could be met by increased bus priority measures, or even trolleybuses, there must be a very high probability that the Uxbridge Road could be ripe for the return of tram route 7 over a partly segregated and a partly street running alignment. If that occurs, then the conversion of the Thames Trains Greenford Branch to light rail might be achieveable relatively cheaply, with track diverted to join Uxbridge Road line via a very short new link at West Ealing. Much of the Heathrow workforce living in Southall, Ealing or Uxbridge could well be enticed onto public transport, if light rail branches can be created to feed into an Uxbridge Road main light rail line. These could fit into mainly open tracts of land to provide a fast segregated link to Heathrow alongside (or down the centre reservation of) routes such as the new A312 road, the M4 link, or perhaps serving the recently pedestrianised Hayes town centre en route.

HEATHROW ORBITAL EXPRESS

'Links from Heathrow towards Uxbridge, Harrow and Kingston. Also distribution around the airport sites; to improve the modal share of public transport in an area of heavy car usage; to improve local public transport links to town centres.'

Peoplemovers may feature as a solution for internal transport within the airport, whilst busways were a probability to enhance public transport perception along some local corridors. However, if the Uxbridge Road Tramway becomes a reality, this would considerably increase the viability of light rail for some of the Heathrow proposals which could link into that.

BRENT CROSS, EDGWARE ROAD AND THE A5 CORRIDOR

'To provide improved links from Brent Cross to the Northern Line and Edgware Road; to assist in the development of the Cricklewood railways yards site; to provide higher quality public transport along the A5 Edgware Road.'

This could involve short distance peoplemovers around the Brent Cross/Cricklewood sites, although clearly a broader scheme may be served by light rail throughout, perhaps extending to central London, and maybe calling for the dust to be blown off from Tim Runnacles' drawings of Marble Arch trackwork proposals? Unlike Uxbridge Road, the Edgware Road does not offer long stretches of wide road or dual carriageway and some serious restraint on other traffic will have to be accepted if street tramway is to be laid along much of it.

WOOD GREEN TOWN CENTRE AND ORBITAL LINKS

'Links across Wood Green to Tottenham, Northumberland Park, Muswell Hill and Crouch End; to improve public transport quality.'

Realistically, light rail would be physically difficult with the possible exception of the former Finsbury Park to Alexandra Palace rail corridor. Somewhat surprisingly, no suggestion was made to include the trunk north-south route 29 corridor (cited in the 1994 CILT report) which could be a likely street tramway candidate.

BARKING REACH AND EXTENSIONS

'To provide services which encourage public transport orientated development at Barking Reach; to extend such a network to provide higher-quality public transport in the Barking area; possibly to improve public transport access to Barking town centre.'

Studies had already suggested a tramway between Barking and Barking Reach as well as to Beckton, although there was no direct mention of Ilford here, which is far and away the major local local shopping centre. A line was shown on the map shooting from the eastern end of the Barking Reach development site northwards to connect with the Underground at Dagenham Heathway.

ROMFORD AREA SCHEME

'Links to Romford from Rainham development area, Harold Hill and Collier Row; to improve public transport quality; to enable better penetration by public transport of Romford town centre; to provide services which encourage public transport oriented development at Rainham; to improve local links.'

The size and phasing of any Rainham development was unclear, but based on Romford alone, light rail was always an unlikely contender.

SUMMARY

The closing chapter of the report stated that the study results would provide a basis for the evaluation of intermediate mode proposals with guidance as to what types of scheme are more likely to be a success in different locations and circumstances, thus drawing up a yardstick or template against which all future schemes would be evaluated. Private sector participation and the co-operation of local authorities was viewed as vital to realise these schemes, and the report was confident that with commitment and funding all could be operational by the year 2000.

TRAMS ACROSS CENTRAL LONDON?

Until very recently, any suggestion of this would have been purely fantasy! After all, even the original London tramway system could only manage this at one point, and then only by constructing the Kingsway tram subway. However, as light rail becomes the prestigious 'new' form of transport for a leading European city to be seen to employ, attitudes are changing. There is still the unanswered question of how to handle the influx of passengers arriving from the expanded heavy rail termini at King's Cross St Pancras, and it has been said many times that the Underground is bursting at the seams at that point.

In 1994, a CILT (Centre for Independent Transport Research in London) report examined the concept of street tramways for cities and central London in particular. It examined costs and benefits, and drew up a case for converting the current 24 and 29 bus routes into tramways. Ambitious the report may have been, but there was much in it that could evolve into reality given the right push from those with the right influence and financial interest.

Early in 1995, an approach was made to London Transport by Westminster Council to examine the possibility of tramway installation along certain very famous corridors. Some ideas arose from of radical pedestrianisation plans, others from how to cater for a greatly expanded movement along an already busy corridor. Many more questions would need to be asked and answered before trams cross central London, but the germ of an idea was there.

On 4th May 1995 *The Guardian* newspaper carried a brief note about Westminster Council's plans suggesting a 'streetcar' (why on earth the Americanisation had crept in nobody knows!) scheme between St Pancras and Waterloo via the Aldwych/Strand area. It spoke of hoped – for 'millennium funding' to boost private investment in the scheme, and of joint venture with Lambeth and Southwark Councils on tram plans. The proposals warranted further mention in the Independent on 6th June 1995 and a subsequent television news slot that same evening, suggesting that the line would run between Kings Cross and the Elephant & Castle. 'In the October 1995 London Transport publication *Planning London's Transport*, tentative mention was made of the central London tram concept as:- 'In some places, there may be sufficient numbers of passengers to justify higher capacity trams or buses running mainly on dedicated parts of the highway with priority at junctions. Such a scheme is currently being looked at for a route between Waterloo and Euston.' Interest in the scheme subsequently blossomed into a Cross-River Partnership involving affected local borough councils, local business interests and London Transport, which then started to develop detailed design for a tramway on the suggested alignment.

AND WHERE NEXT?

Whilst London tramway interest at the end of the 1990s focused on the early operation of the basic Croydon Tramlink system, background work was slowly evolving on extension plans (see pages 68 and 69) and on ideas for tramways elsewhere in the capital. Following distillation from the *New Ideas for Public Transport In Outer London* reports and the embryonic 'Cross River Partnership' central tramway plan, London Transport issued four leaflets indicating an intention to work towards realisation of 'intermediate mode schemes'. These floated ideas for four schemes, none of which were mode-specific, but suggesting a range of possible modes from guided bus through trolleybus to tram on three of these. Tram was no longer mentioned as a possible mode in the case of the 'East London Transit', which looked at an extensive bus/trolleybus based scheme from Barking/Ilford across to Romford and its environs.

The suggested lines with tram as a possible mode were:

Greenwich Waterfront Transit – a line from Abbey Wood via Thamesmead, Woolwich, Lower Charlton and the North Greenwich peninsula to Greenwich Station.

Uxbridge Road Transit – a line from Uxbridge via Southall, Ealing and Acton to Shepherds Bush – a suggested revival of former tram route 7!

Cross River Transit – a line from Camden Town via Euston, Kingsway, Waterloo, and Elephant to Peckham Rye Railway Station. Additionally, a spur from Euston terminated at a location named as 'Kings Cross North' and a south-western branch broke away at Waterloo to serve Kennington and Stockwell.

All of these schemes received extensive local press coverage and even the East London package was often referred to in the press as a 'tram proposal', although the early decision had been taken to exclude the offer of trams for that scheme.

At the same time, some tentative proposals were under review for extending Croydon Tramlink as its operation period started. Various suggestions gained press coverage, sometimes without foundation. As soon as the government go-ahead for the initial Tramlink scheme had been given in 1996, Croydon Council published its desires to see Tramlink extended further into the Purley Way retail park, Thornton Heath, Purley and Crystal Palace. Whilst no specifics were settled upon, initial reviews were carried out with the aim of serving Crystal Palace, Purley Way, the A23 corridor and Sutton by tram.

Following the election of Ken Livingstone as London Mayor in May 2000, a Draft Transport Strategy for London was published. This was subsequently followed by a firmed up document in June 2001. Politically, an important emphasis was towards traffic reduction throughout London with the need to make public transport a more attractive alternative to private transport as vital to this policy. It was now politically acceptable to suggest reallocation of roadspace as part of the exercise to make public transport more reliable. Two important key aims expressed in the documents were to propose a congestion-charging scheme for central London and to invest heavily in measures to improve bus services throughout the capital. Both documents praised the successes of the DLR and Croydon Tramlink. They included as policy items pledges to examine Tramlink extension possibilities and to pursue the four 'intermediate mode' proposals towards a point where the Mayor would have sufficient information to hand to make early decisions on which if any schemes should proceed towards realisation.

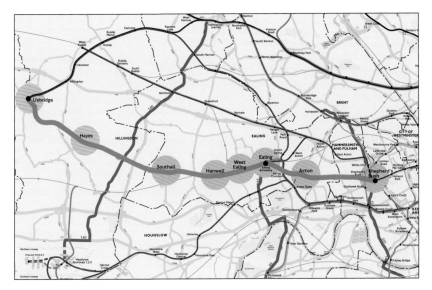

Computer generated view of a tram at Ealing Town Hall on the proposed Uxbridge Road route.

In 2001, Transport for London started to issue further documentation for public consumption giving a clearer outline to the proposals. An initial stage of public consultation was launched in July 2001 for the East London and Greenwich schemes, with that for Uxbridge Road (now marketed as West London Transit) and Cross River following in the Autumn. Questionnaires were distributed to interested parties, seeking public opinion and probing into aspects which might cause public concern over the schemes. Mode preferences were asked for on the questionnaire, although tram was not given as a choice on the East London scheme.

By this time, the Greenwich scheme was being offered as a two-stage event, with phase one now suggesting a 'transit' corridor as far west only as North Greenwich Station, with route variants in the Woolwich Arsenal area. Much of the alignment was street based, often suggesting occupation by 'transit' of one part of what were at the time dual carriageway roads. It is interesting to note that any suggestion of 'guided' bus had now disappeared from all publicity items, with the only guided vehicles on offer for three of the schemes now being tram. All bus and trolleybus options would now be manually steered. It is reasonable to assume that disillusionment with guided buses had stemmed from abortive trials carried out with under-road electronically guided buses during 1999 on a short stretch of the Greenwich alignment.

The Cross River Transit alignment offered for public consultation differed slightly from that shown in the earlier leaflet. Its south eastern leg was now shown to terminate at Peckham Bus Station, whilst the south western leg now went beyond Stockwell to terminate at Brixton. Whilst the mode was still nominally open to debate, some publicity now described the scheme as 'The London Tram'. A predicted annual patronage of 72 million would suggest trams as the only mode capable of shifting such numbers.

Likely patronage predictions of 50 million per annum also point towards tram as a buoyant candidate for 'West London Transit'.

Less concrete information was publicly available in 2001 surrounding Tramlink extension proposals beyond arrows on a map, but there are few logical variations available if the destinations suggested by the Mayor's Strategy document are to be reached. The route to Sutton could connect into the existing line to Wimbledon either in the Morden Road or Mitcham areas, either of which suggests highway alignment between Sutton and St Helier. Between St Helier and line 1 of the present tramway, wide roads leave room for a tramway along a number of alternative alignments. North and south of Croydon, traffic calming may permit trams to use streets as the most direct route towards Purley and Norbury. Reaching Crystal Palace could present a greater challenge, with some utilisation of rail corridor having been implied to date. It is likely that details will become clearer if any of the proposals move on to a public consultation stage similar to that reached by the 'intermediate mode' schemes.

In 2001, the future for the tram in London looked optimistic. If Cross-River Transit materialises as a tramway, all remaining taboos surrounding trams in London will have been shattered and TfL will have achieved that surface line across the heart of the capital so elusive to first generation tramway promoters. There will be then be no barriers to what can be achieved in the future as expansion proposals for CRT inevitably arise for scrutiny. Perhaps CRT will push beyond Brixton eventually linking up to Croydon Tramlink and will those Runnacles plans for complex tramway junctions at places like Marble Arch eventually find a purpose?

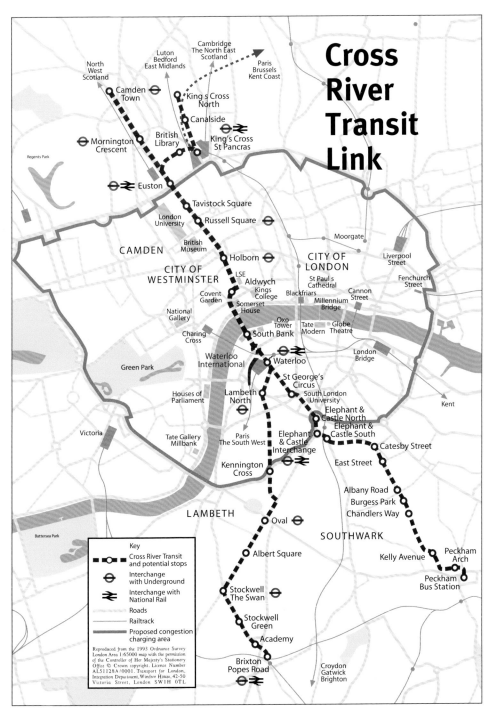

Cross River Transit Link

Key

- ▪▪◉▪▪ Cross River Transit and potential stops
- ⊖ Interchange with Underground
- ⇌ Interchange with National Rail
- Roads
- Railtrack
- Proposed congestion charging area

Reproduced from the 1993 Ordnance Survey London Area 1:65000 map with the permission of the Controller of Her Majesty's Stationery Office © Crown copyright. Licence Number ALS1128A/0001. Transport for London, Integration Department, Windsor House, 42-50 Victoria Street, London SW1H 0TL

North West Scotland

Camden Town
Luton Bedford East Midlands
Cambridge The North East Scotland
Paris Brussels Kent Coast
King's Cross North
Canalside
Mornington Crescent
British Library
King's Cross St Pancras
Euston
Tavistock Square
London University
Russell Square
Moorgate
Liverpool Street
CAMDEN
British Museum
Holborn
CITY OF LONDON
Fenchurch Street
CITY OF WESTMINSTER
LSE Aldwych
Kings College
Covent Garden
Somerset House
St Paul's Cathedral
Blackfriars
Cannon Street
Millennium Bridge
National Gallery
Charing Cross
Oxo Tower
South Bank
Tate Modern
Globe Theatre
Waterloo International
Waterloo
London Bridge
Green Park
St George's Circus
South London University
Houses of Parliament
Lambeth North
Elephant & Castle North
Kent
Victoria
Tate Gallery Millbank
Paris The South West
Elephant & Castle Interchange
Elephant & Castle South
Catesby Street
Kennington Cross
East Street
Albany Road
Burgess Park
Chandlers Way
LAMBETH
Oval
SOUTHWARK
Battersea Park
Albert Square
Kelly Avenue
Peckham Arch
Peckham Bus Station
Stockwell The Swan
Stockwell Green
Academy
Brixton Popes Road
Croydon Gatwick Brighton

Regents Park

MANCHESTER METROLINK

The origins of the Manchester Metrolink system lie in the failure of a previous project, the Picc-Vic scheme. That scheme was drawn up in the 1970s and would have provided a heavy rail tunnel under Manchester linking the city's two main railway stations, Piccadilly and Victoria. Suburban rail services would have been joined together to run across the city centre in a similar way to the Merseyrail 'loop and link' system, which was devised and built in the same era. Manchester was however unable to secure the funding for Picc-Vic and the scheme was dropped.

There was still a wish on the part of Greater Manchester PTE (GMPTE) to link the city's two main stations and to upgrade suburban rail lines and a Rail Study Group involving BR and Greater Manchester Council was set up in 1982 to investigate alternative (and less costly) options. The study group visited many overseas cities, both on the Continent and in the US, to view light rail and guided bus schemes that were already up and running (there being no modern light rail systems in the UK at that time). Their conclusion was that light rail offered the best solution. The vehicles were quiet and pollution free, they could be fully accessible to the mobility-impaired and moreover light rail was a proven winner in encouraging the motorist out of his or her car and onto public transport. Guided bus offered some of the attributes of light rail in terms of speed, frequency and the use of a reserved right of way but it had an image problem as far as motorists were concerned and pollution from the vehicles would be an issue in the city centre.

PLANNING

GMPTE studied the local rail network to see which lines could be converted to light rail operation (the option of building new lines to open up new corridors, mooted in the 1960s with a north–south Langley to Wythenshawe proposal, was regrettably not pursued on cost grounds). Two lines immediately presented themselves as front runners, those to Altrincham and Bury. Neither carried much in the way of freight traffic (apart from at the south end of the Altrincham line, which could be segregated) and, more importantly, neither carried long-distance InterCity services. The Altrincham line carried a local service to Chester but that could be diverted between Manchester and Altrincham on an alternative route via Stockport, which would also have the beneficial effect of providing a direct rail service between Stockport and Altrincham for the first time since 1931. The two lines were BR's busiest suburban lines in the Manchester area, carrying between them 6 million passengers a year, but both suffered from poor penetration of the city centre – Metrolink, as the proposed light rail system came to be known, would cure that.

A scheme was devised to link the Altrincham and Bury lines by means of street running in the centre of Manchester. There would also be a branch from Piccadilly Gardens to Piccadilly station, where Metrolink would terminate in the 'Undercroft' beneath the main station. The total route mileage of the initial system would be 19 miles. The scheme would make use of the disused viaduct approach into the former Manchester Central station (closed in May 1969 and by now converted into the G-Mex exhibition centre) as a means of segregating the Metrolink Altrincham line from the former Cheshire Lines Committee main line to Liverpool via Warrington Central. That service, which had previously used Manchester Central as its terminus, had already been diverted to reach Piccadilly via Oxford Road, and so the Altrincham and Liverpool services were effectively to swap routes.

The first Bill to authorise construction of the system was deposited in Parliament in November 1984. In March 1987 GMPTE set up a light rail demonstration at Debdale Park, on the east side of Manchester adjacent to Hyde Road Junction on the Fallowfield loop freight-only line. A temporary wooden platform was built and London Docklands car No.11 (fitted with a pantograph for the event) gave public rides along a mile and a quarter section of electrified line to a point just beyond the former Reddish maintenance depot. Remaining overhead supports from the former Manchester–Sheffield–Wath electrification were used for the demonstration along with new 'typhoon-proof' supports to the same design as those provided for then recently-built Tuen Mun system in Hong Kong. Power was provided by a class 303 former Glasgow Blue Train electric multiple-unit, which acted as a transformer to convert 25kV ac from the Hadfield line to the required 750v dc. The demonstration proved popular and helped to show light rail as a concept to the general public and politicians alike. The two key attributes which the demonstration highlighted were accessibility (there was level boarding from the platform) and good acceleration.

The then Conservative government sat on the proposals for a number of years and Secretary of State for Transport Nicholas Ridley was quoted as being sceptical of the scheme's potential to attract motorists out of their cars. The scheme had to overcome a number of obstacles including bus deregulation and the abolition of the Greater Manchester Council in May 1986. However the PTE was able to overcome all of these and outline funding approval for the scheme was finally given in January 1988. The Government insisted that the scheme be built using a 'DBOM' (Design, Build, Operate and Maintain) contract whereby the private sector would carry out all four of those functions. GMPTE maintained that it would be cheaper for Metrolink to be built and operated by the public sector, as the successful Tyne & Wear PTE Metro had been, but the GMPTA accepted this in the interests of progress. Tenders were invited and the successful one was from the GMA consortium, consisting of GEC Alsthom, GM Buses, John Mowlem and Amec. The initial operating concession was to be for 15 years, although later events were to reduce that period significantly.

GMPTE won an important victory in securing the right to specify the service level and hours of operation of the system, although this was at the expense of relinquishing any control over fare levels. The PTE was only able to specify the concessionary flat fare for pensioners, which would entail support payments being made to the concesionnaire so that they were no better or worse off than if the concessionary fare scheme did not exist. A downside of the conversion of two former BR lines to Metrolink was that only Greater Manchester residents would now qualify for discounted travel. Holders of senior and other national railcards including the disabled persons railcard would suddenly find that they had to pay full fare unless they qualified for a GMPTE pass. However the ability for wheelchair users to simply 'turn up and go' on Metrolink as opposed to having to give 24 or 48 hours' notice was a compensation.

Cyclists were also less than pleased that they would no longer be able to take their bikes with them, the carriage of cycles not being allowed on Metrolink.

Not everyone was happy with the choice of light rail for Manchester. The Greater Manchester Transport Action Group (GMTAG), one of whose leading members had played a key role in the development of the Merseyrail loop and link project, petitioned the House of Lords in an attempt to have the project stopped in favour of a tunnel-based heavy rail solution. The group also used the local press to further their campaign, which ultimately (and happily for the future of light rail in the UK) proved unsuccessful. It has to be said that the Manchester Evening News has been and still is consistently supportive of Metrolink, a factor which must have helped to persuade local politicians and public opinion in general to support the scheme. Such support has not been forthcoming everywhere in the UK, most notably in Sheffield.

CONSTRUCTION

Construction began in March 1989 with the diversion of services such as telephone and electricity cables and gas, water, drainage and sewage pipes from under the alignment in the city centre. This was so that Metrolink services would not be disrupted in the event of any of these services needing to be accessed and it inevitably caused considerable disruption for pedestrians, motorists and bus passengers. More use could have been made of modern overseas tramway practice during this period.

The Manchester–Altrincham–Chester rail service was diverted to run via Stockport in May 1989 as part of the new 'Windsor Link' timetable but this also paved the way for Metrolink conversion of the Altrincham line. Conversion work started on both the Bury and Altrincham lines whilst the BR trains were still running but the final BR train ran on the Bury line on 16th August 1991 and on the Altrincham line on 24th December 1991. In both cases there were emotional scenes as the last respects were paid and much exploding of detonators beneath the trains' wheels. Buses were to replace the rail service on both lines until Metrolink began.

Conversion work could now begin in earnest on both lines. On the Bury line the redundant and life-expired 1200v dc third rail had to be removed and overhead electrification had to be installed. Work on the Altrincham line involved the conversion of the overhead supply from 25kV ac to 750v dc, the construction of a diveunder at Cornbrook to take Metrolink under the Liverpool line and the building of an electrified tramway on the course of the former CLC line into Manchester Central. Bridges on that section needed much attention as they had had virtually none since Central station had closed 22 years earlier. One bridge span, at Cornbrook, was completely replaced and the bridge over the

Castlefield Junction to Ordsall Lane Junction line was refurbished and raised to provide clearance for electrification of the line below (which at the time of writing has still to take place). Two-aspect signalling was installed on the reserved track sections of both the Altrincham and Bury lines. The Altrincham line had previously had four-aspect signalling and the Bury line had been largely controlled by semaphores. The section of line between Deansgate Junction (south of Timperley) and Altrincham had already been remodelled and resignalled by BR in July 1991 in preparation for Metrolink and remained under its control.

Much work was required to improve access for mobility-impaired people at stations along both lines. Where there was room, sloping ramps were provided as a low-tech and reliable solution. Where this was not possible lifts were installed. A dedicated wheelchair boarding and alighting point had to be created on each platform and at some stations this entailed the creation of a slightly raised section of platform which protruded towards the point where the appropriate doors of the vehicle would stop. This was to guarantee level access to the vehicle without a significant gap. Ticket vending machines (TVMs) had to be installed as all of the stations would be unmanned and many CCTV cameras were provided so that the control centre at Queens Road, Manchester, could monitor what was happening at stations.

Queens Road, to the north of the city centre, was also the location chosen for the maintenance depot and is equipped with a wheel lathe, a wheel press, jacks, an overhead crane, an electrical repair shop and a bogie maintenance area. Only vehicles with serious accident damage need to be sent away for repair. The successful tenderer only provided 26 vehicles for the initial system, despite the fact that GMPTE were of the view that 36 were required if the system was to realise its full potential. This was partly because the then Department of Transport and the Treasury failed to take account of the very large number of additional passengers that Metrolink would generate over and above the numbers previously carried on the Altrincham and Bury lines.

Tracklaying in progress on High Street in Manchester City Centre.

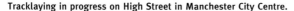

Soon the street-running alignment of Metrolink in the city centre was taking shape with its distinctive profiled platforms. A full-length high platform was provided at Piccadilly Gardens but this was ruled to be out of the question at other locations in the city centre, in particular the sensitive site adjacent to the Cenotaph in St Peters Square (in the event the profiled platforms at Market Street and High Street were both replaced by a single, full-length high platform in Market Street on 10th August 1998). Problems were encountered on Mosley Street with the breaking up of the polymer, which is used to keep the rails in place. This was due partly to the pounding that the track received from buses passing along it and partly to the failure to protect the polymer from moisture whilst it was hardening. The contractors had to revisit the site several times before a lasting solution was found.

There was much adverse comment over the number and intrusiveness of traction poles and associated equipment in the city centre (they are painted black). Criticism came notably from Lord St John of Fawsley, the Chairman of the Royal Fine Arts Commission. The PTE cited a refusal by some owners of adjoining buildings to allow the overhead lines to be attached to their buildings, which would have eliminated the need for many of the poles. Manchester City Council's own Town Hall and Central Library buildings in the pole-cluttered St Peters Square have somehow been excused having any tramway wires attached to them, in contrast to established practice at prestigious locations abroad.

People often ask why Metrolink was not designed and built as a low-platform system, which would have made disabled access easier and has now become the norm for new systems. The reasons for this were several. Firstly low-floor vehicle technology was in its infancy when Phase 1 of Metrolink was being developed. Secondly the vehicles would have been much more expensive, and thirdly much expenditure would have been required in demolishing the high platforms at the former BR stations, which formed by far the majority of the Phase 1 stations.

Vehicle 1010 *Manchester Champion* **alongside G-Mex on the occasion of the Royal opening of Metrolink on Friday 17th July 1992. Note the white wheel surrounds and the Royal Standard flying from the roof of the vehicle on which the Queen travelled from St Peters Square to Bury.**

The first unit on test at Piccadilly.

THE TRAMS

The vehicles, numbered 1001–26, were built in Italy by Firema (now Ansaldo Firema) and transported to Manchester by low loader, the bodies being transported separately from the bogies after difficulties were encountered in transporting the first vehicle as a complete unit. Each tram is mounted on three bogies, two motored and a centre, unmotored bogie, which carries the articulation. The trams, which are of Firema type T68, have a seating capacity of 82 plus four tip-up seats and two wheelchair spaces. There is room for 122 standing passengers (at 4 per square metre). The trams are 2.65 metres wide (at the time very wide for street-running vehicles) and have a quoted maximum speed of 80km/h or around 50mph.

The fact that the vehicles were built in Italy caused much comment at the time, many people believing that they should have been built in the UK. The PTE countered by saying that the issue was a matter for the GMA consortium and that no UK manufacturer could build the vehicles to the required specification within the requisite timescale. In the event much work was required on the trams before they could be used for test running and driver training. There were particular problems with the internal wiring and vehicle 1014 initially became a 'Christmas Tree' for spares to keep the remainder of the fleet running. A Special Purpose Vehicle (SPV) was provided for the system by the then RFS Industries of Doncaster. The primary function of this vehicle, which is diesel-powered and equipped with a crane, is vehicle recovery but it can be also be used for a host of other purposes including inspection and repair of the overhead line equipment and attention to lineside structures. The shortfall in vehicle numbers has produced severe overcrowding and overflow at peak periods as only a small number of services can be strengthened to operate with trams in coupled pairs.

1007 at Victoria station on 27th April 1992.

SERVICES BEGIN

The first section of Metrolink to open to the public was between Victoria station and Bury on 6th April 1992. Passengers were initially somewhat baffled by the ticket machines, particularly as you had to discover which zone your destination was in before approaching the machine. The fares came as something of a surprise as well, being higher than the previous subsidised BR fares. Red carnations were handed to each female passenger on the first day. Monday 27th April 1992 saw the inauguration of the first section of a modern street-running tram system in the UK, between Victoria station and G-Mex. Vehicle 1007 was chosen to inaugurate this section as that had been the number of Manchester's last tram on 10th January 1949. The vehicle carried the same headboard as had been carried in 1949.

Monday 15th June 1992 saw the opening of the section between G-Mex and Altrincham and that town's one-legged town crier was there to greet the first tram.

Various BR worthies were also in attendance as Metrolink uses BR (now Railtrack) metals between Deansgate Junction (Timperley) and Altrincham. The final section of Metrolink to open was the short branch from Piccadilly Gardens to Piccadilly Station, on 20th July 1992. Her Majesty the Queen officially opened Metrolink by unveiling a commemorative stone at St Peters Square station on Friday 17th July 1992, after which she travelled to Bury in vehicle 1010. The vehicle flew the Royal Standard above the cab and boasted white wheel surrounds for the occasion.

Unfortunately it had not proved possible to carry out much work at the former BR stations due to a shortage of funds and passengers had to make do with squalid conditions for a number of years after opening. Most of the glass in the footbridge at Stretford station on the Altrincham line was smashed by vandals in the years following Metrolink conversion and GMPTE was eventually able to fund demolition of the bridge and its replacement by separate concrete steps to each platform. However this station is still at the time of writing (September 2001) in need of much more shelter and the whole Metrolink system lacks any public art such as that found on the Midland Metro or on new continental systems such as Strasbourg. A quality public transport system needs and deserves quality waiting areas if it is to be an attractive alternative to the car.

OPERATION

In terms of patronage Metrolink became an instant success and chronic over-crowding was soon a feature at peak periods. A less predictable development was the great increase in off-peak patronage with many passengers (especially pensioners) making the full trip from Altrincham to Bury and vice versa. It was soon necessary to extend the 6-minute peak hour frequency to also operate between the peaks and during Saturday daytime. Coupled pairs are operated on selected peak hour services but this only alleviates the overcrowding to some extent. Some people do not use Metrolink at peak periods because they know that they would not be able to board at stations approaching the city centre. Thus there is latent demand that is not being met and there is currently no spare capacity to cater for the opening of new stations. A plan to install centre sections in 13 of the Phase 1 vehicles (thereby increasing their capacity by 40%) has attracted Government funding but it remains to be seen whether it is feasible. One problem is the fact that the vehicles would be out of service whilst the centre sections were fitted. A simpler, quicker and cheaper solution would be to improve the inadequate standee facilities and to perhaps remove some seats to create more standing space.

A problem which Metrolink has in the city centre is a lack of traffic light priority. It can be infuriating to be approaching (say) Portland Street from Piccadilly station only to see the tram signal protecting the road junction turn to 'stop' in front of you. It says much for the clout of the road lobby in the UK and the pro-road thinking of the then Department of Transport that such an environmentally-friendly, pollution-free and safe form of transport should have to wait for private cars and buses. The situation has however progressively improved to the extent that there are now only two major road junctions where Metrolink does not have traffic light priority.

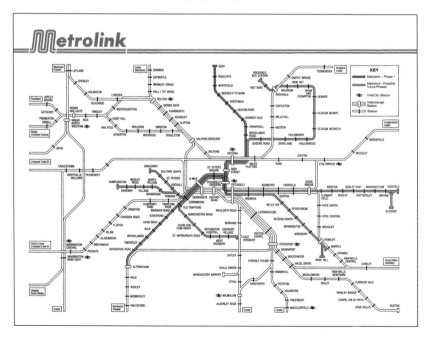

FARES AND TICKETING

Another persistent niggle with Metrolink has been the lack of fare integration with other modes of public transport in Greater Manchester. This problem arose largely because Metrolink was a private operation which was superimposed on a publicly-funded public transport system. Thus the GMPTE range of Travelcards for weekly, monthly and annual use are not valid on Metrolink (even though the PTE actually owns the Metrolink system!) except in the city centre. Also tickets between Altrincham and Manchester have to be either via Metrolink or on heavy rail via Stockport and passengers have to return via the same mode as they have used for their outward journey.

Steps have been taken to improve matters since the system opened. The popular GMPTE Wayfarer bus and rail off-peak day rover ticket was extended to include the whole of the Metrolink system from 1st April 1998 following a change of concessionaire. The PTE also introduced a range of Day Saver tickets on 29th September 1998, which include off-peak travel on Metrolink as well as the bus and rail networks. Metrolink tickets can now be purchased from the rail booking office at Altrincham station, which is of great benefit to those who have difficulty with the ticket machines (or on the frequent occasions when none of the ticket machines is working). However for many, particularly commuters, Metrolink remains an expensive option. The system has the potential to carry far more passengers if four conditions are met: (a) there is much more rolling stock, (b) fares are reduced significantly and tickets are made more easily available, (c) car parking at stations is dramatically improved and (d) there is far stronger promotion of services.

Another positive development was the introduction on 21st March 1999 of an off-peak day rover ticket for the entire Metrolink system. The Metromax ticket currently costs £3.00 and is available from all ticket machines (passengers should press 'Metromax' and 'return'). The ticket is valid after 09.30 on Monday to Friday and all day on Saturdays, Sundays and bank holidays. After much criticism some Metrolink ticket machines were modified to accept bank notes although this has made them much less reliable. Unlike some other UK systems Metrolink has yet to go down the road of employing conductors on its vehicles.

Policing for the Metrolink system is provided by a dedicated squad of 29 Greater Manchester Police officers, who are able to call upon the resources of the remainder of the force at times of emergency. They normally patrol the system in twos but may appear in greater numbers when stations are closed off for ticket checks or when a football match is taking place at Old Trafford.

Broadway station, showing ticket machines and the passenger emergency call units.

SALFORD QUAYS AND ECCLES

In the mid-1990s funding became available for the first extension to the Metrolink system, the four and a half mile branch from Cornbrook (between G-Mex and Trafford Bar stations on the Altrincham line) to Salford Quays and Eccles. The line was intended to help the regeneration of the former Salford Docks area and it was decided to extend the line through to Eccles to provide a town terminus. Some of the funding for Phase 2, as it became known, came from the sale of GM Buses, the PTA's bus company. To proceed with the extension it was necessary to re-tender the contract for the whole Metrolink operation including the Altrincham and Bury lines.

The winning consortium was ALTRAM (which also has the concession for Midland Metro) with Serco Limited becoming the operators of the system as successors to the first operating company Greater Manchester Metro Limited (GMML). Construction of the new line began on 25th April 1997 and the first section, from Cornbrook to Broadway, opened on 6th December 1999. The opening ceremony was performed by none other than the Prime Minister, the Rt Hon Tony Blair MP, who unveiled a poster case at Salford Quays station. The section from Broadway to Eccles, which incorporates much street running, opened on 21st July 2000.

Six new vehicles, Nos 2001–2006, were purchased from Ansaldo Firema for the extension. The vehicles were outwardly very similar to the Phase 1 stock but incorporated interior destination displays and also featured a contrasting colour for the doors to comply with the Disability Discrimination Act. The main mechanical difference was the use of ac traction motors which gives the vehicles a distinctive sound. Three vehicles from the original batch, Nos 1005, 1010 and 1015, were modified with shrouded couplers and fairings over the bogies to enable them to operate on the Eccles line (the protruding coupler was never liked by the Railway Inspectorate, which considered it unsafe for street running amongst ordinary traffic).

Ansaldo 2004 on the first section of the extension to Eccles, photographed in January 2000.

A park and ride site, with space for 450 cars, was opened at Ladywell on the Eccles line on 13th August 2001. The site features CCTV surveillance and parking was initially free as an introductory offer. The initial prediction was that the Eccles line would carry 6 million passengers a year but this was subsequently reduced to 4 million. The opening of the Lowry Centre (near to Harbour City station) in 2000 boosted the line's carryings but at the time of writing off-peak patronage has yet to really take off. This is due partly to the meandering nature of the route, which often means that it is cheaper and quicker to make the journey by bus. Two highway improvements straddling the new line were inaugurated just before the new line opened, further improving the attractiveness of competing road alternatives into the city centre from both Salford Quays and Eccles.

Above **Interior view of one of the latest batch of trams for Metrolink.**

Left **Heaton Park station showing lift towers added for the tram service.**

FUTURE PLANS

What of the future? The success of Phase 1 of Metrolink encouraged the PTE to pursue extensions to the system and it was decided to lump these together in a single contract approach. The thinking was that it would be cheaper to build a number of extensions at the same time rather than in a piecemeal fashion. The *Manchester Evening News* helped considerably in the campaign for the single contract, including hiring a light plane to trail a banner saying 'Don't forget Manchester Metrolink' which flew over the opening ceremony for the Midland Metro performed by the Princess Royal.

In March 2000 the Government gave the go ahead for the single contract, which included lines from Piccadilly to Ashton via the Commonwealth Games stadium, Trafford Bar to Manchester Airport via Chorlton (with a loop around the sprawling Wythenshawe estate) and Victoria to Rochdale town centre via Oldham town centre (largely on the existing rail alignment). Bidders for Phase 3, as the single contract became known, would also have the opportunity to quote for a branch to the Lowry Centre and a line from Pomona (on the Eccles line) to the Trafford Centre (an out-of-town shopping centre). However public funding would not be available for the branch to the Trafford Centre. A line from Hough End (Chorlton) to Stockport via East Didsbury was later added to the list of lines for which the bidders would have the opportunity to provide a quotation following strong public support for an extension to Stockport.

Phase 3 would also incorporate a second depot (solely for stabling, routine maintenance and cleaning) and it was decided to site this alongside the Altrincham line between Trafford Bar and Old Trafford stations. Access would also be available to and from the Airport/Stockport line. The initial depot, where all heavy maintenance would still be carried out, would not have the capacity to deal with the additional vehicles for Phase 3 (a figure of 62 was quoted).

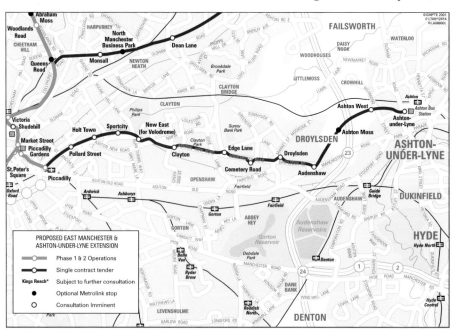

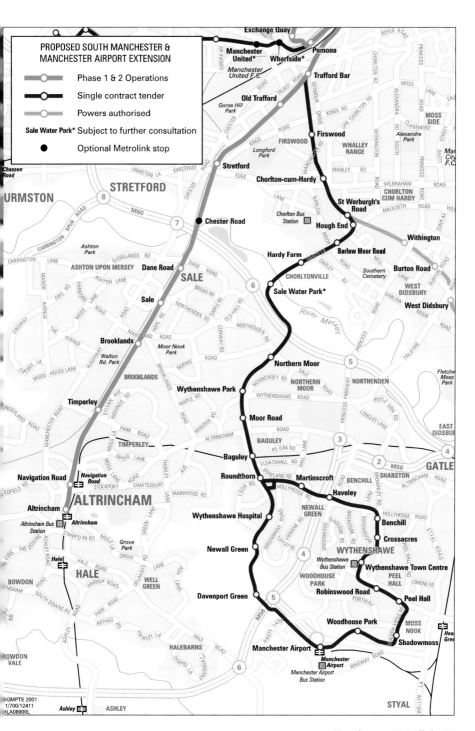

PROPOSED SOUTH MANCHESTER &
MANCHESTER AIRPORT EXTENSION

Phase 1 & 2 Operations
Single contract tender
Powers authorised
Sale Water Park* Subject to further consultation
● Optional Metrolink stop

The order in which the Phase 3 lines will be built is a matter for the winning consortium. There was great disappointment when it was announced that the line from Piccadilly station to the Commonwealth Games stadium (part of the future Ashton route) would not be ready in time for the Games, which begin on 25th July 2002. Current plans are for the contract for Phase 3 to be awarded in late 2002 with construction work beginning in early 2003. Opening of the new lines will take place from 2006 onwards.

Looking beyond Phase 3, other extensions have been suggested by the South East Manchester Multi-Modal Study (SEMMS) including a link from Stockport to Wythenshawe partly using a rail alignment and a line from Stockport to Marple, which would use the rail alignment between Romiley and Rose Hill. First Group have suggested a 'TramTrain' concept whereby light rail vehicles would run on heavy rail lines from (say) Wigan and then access the street tracks in the centre of Manchester to provide city centre penetration. This would require a second cross-city Metrolink line to provide the additional capacity required (a second cross-city line will probably also be needed to provide capacity for the Trafford Centre and Stockport lines).

Metrolink has undoubtedly been a success. The numbers using the Bury and Altrincham lines have risen from 6 million a year to about 14 million and the Eccles line is carrying in excess of 2 million passengers a year. Some 20% of Metrolink users are former car users, who have been attracted onto quality public transport by Metrolink's winning combination of frequency, accessibility and good city centre penetration. By its success Metrolink has demonstrated the case for other light rail systems in the UK and the system can be clearly seen as a trailblazer for the rebirth of tramways in the UK.

One of the second series cars outbound to Eccles crossing the bowstring girder bridge over Great Bridgewater Street alongside G-Mex. The design of the bridge echoes the shape of the roof of G-Mex.

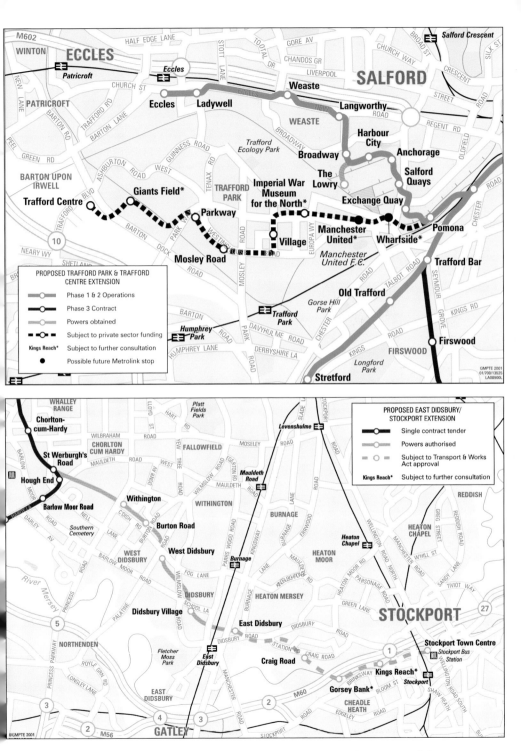

PROPOSED TRAFFORD PARK & TRAFFORD CENTRE EXTENSION

- Phase 1 & 2 Operations
- Phase 3 Contract
- Powers obtained
- Subject to private sector funding
- Kings Reach* Subject to further consultation
- Possible future Metrolink stop

M602
WINTON
ECCLES
HALF EDGE LANE
Patricroft
Eccles
CHURCH ST
PATRICROFT
Eccles
Ladywell
Weaste
SALFORD
Salford Crescent
WEASTE
Langworthy
Harbour City
BARTON UPON IRWELL
Giants Field*
Trafford Ecology Park
Broadway
Anchorage
Trafford Centre
TRAFFORD PARK
Imperial War Museum for the North*
The Lowry
Salford Quays
Parkway
Exchange Quay
10
Manchester United*
Wharfside*
Pomona
Mosley Road
Village
Manchester United F.C.
Trafford Bar
NEARY WY
Old Trafford
Gorse Hill Park
Firswood
Trafford Park
Humphrey Park
Stretford
Longford Park
FIRSWOOD
GMPTE 2001
01/700/13525
LA08900L

PROPOSED EAST DIDSBURY/ STOCKPORT EXTENSION

- Single contract tender
- Powers authorised
- Subject to Transport & Works Act approval
- Kings Reach* Subject to further consultation

WHALLEY RANGE
Chorlton-cum-Hardy
Platt Fields Park
Levenshulme
St Werburgh's Road
CHORLTON CUM HARDY
FALLOWFIELD
MOSELEY
REDDISH
Hough End
WITHINGTON
Mauldeth Road
BURNAGE
HEATON CHAPEL
Withington
Barlow Moor Road
Burton Road
Heaton Chapel
Southern Cemetery
WEST DIDSBURY
West Didsbury
Burnage
HEATON MOOR
River Mersey
DIDSBURY
HEATON MERSEY
STOCKPORT
Didsbury Village
5
East Didsbury
NORTHENDEN
Fletcher Moss Park
East Didsbury
Craig Road
Stockport Town Centre
Stockport Bus Station
Kings Reach*
Stockport
EAST DIDSBURY
Gorsey Bank*
3
CHEADLE HEATH
M60
GATLEY
M56
©GMPTE 2001

MIDLAND METRO

The idea of reintroducing trams to the West Midlands can be traced back to the early 1950s, in fact just eighteen months after the closure of Birmingham City Transport's last tram routes. In December 1954 Alderman W T Bowen, Chairman of the city's General Purposes Committee, given the job of coming up with a solution to the ever worsening traffic congestion, put forward a scheme to reintroduce trams on the former Bristol Road and Tyburn Road routes. Alderman Bowen saw this as the first two lines of a network that would gradually be built along all the main approaches to the city. New roads would be constructed with central reservations for the trams and a subway would be provided in the city centre. A 5-man deputation from the City Council visited the East Coast of the USA and the city of Philadelphia convinced them that a totally segregated rapid transit system was necessary. At that stage Birmingham was just commencing the building of its Inner Ring Road and in 1957 the City Council decided the cost of a rapid transit system, at £14m, could not be justified at that time and the idea would be deferred until 1963.

In 1964 the Ministry of Transport and the local authorities commissioned consultants Freeman Fox, Wilbur Smith & Associates to produce a report on transport in the West Midlands conurbation. Called the West Midlands Transportation Study, a preliminary report was issued in 1967 which identified that new roads were rapidly being saturated soon after opening and that fixed track systems should be looked at for the most heavily used corridors.

The result of this was that the City Council and the Ministry of Transport commissioned De Leuw, Chadwick, O'hEocha to look at the potential for developing rapid transit in Birmingham with special reference to the Redditch-city centre–Sutton Coldfield (A38) corridor. A branch to Chelmsley Wood, a new residential area with a population of some 60,000 was also included. Both bus, sharing road space with other vehicles and on its own right-of-way, and rail, in the form of upgraded suburban services or a new rapid transit system, were evaluated. The study concluded that by 1981 four corridors would have a high patronage, namely:

- Lichfield–Sutton Coldfield–Birmingham–Redditch (A38).
- Birmingham–Shirley–Solihull (A34 south).
- Birmingham–Chelmsley Wood (A45).
- Birmingham–Wolverhampton (A41).

The first corridor would involve upgrading the existing railway lines, electrifying them and creating a new alignment under the city centre. The next two would be served by a new underground system but the A41 corridor proposals saw the former Great Western Railway from Birmingham Snow Hill to Wolverhampton via Wednesbury, then being run down, being converted to a segregated busway. Services along this alignment would use the busway for short sections on routes linking the many towns along the way.

The plans disappeared into the reorganisation of local government that took place at the end of the 1960s and the beginning of the 1970s. One of the effects of this reorganisation was the creation of passenger transport authorities, and later executives, that co-ordinated and invested in public transport systems. In the West Midlands the Authority took responsibility for a number of under-used railways and gradually developed these, slowly but surely increasing traffic. The Snow Hill to Wolverhampton line, however, closed to passengers in March 1972.

The Passenger Transport Authority developed a co-ordinated bus and rail system, but whilst rail traffic gradually rose bus patronage fell at an increasing rate. Central government was funding services that were less effective each year.

NEW APPROACHES

In late 1978 the UK, along with other countries, suffered a petroleum energy shortage, caused by the fall of the Shah's regime in Iran, and the effects of this were not lost on James Isaacs who had been appointed Director General of the PTE that year. In April 1979 he presented a report prepared jointly with the County Surveyor on alternative energy sources for public transport. This was followed the next year when Isaacs, reporting that the integrated public transport system was nearly complete, also advised the PTE to look at alternatives for motive power. However it was not until July 1981 that, as part of a report entitled 'Policy for development of the local rail system' Isaacs wrote:

'Members will be aware of the Newcastle (Tyne & Wear) metro system which has recently been opened and is still due for further expansion. This system is based on British Rail lines to the standards of a heavy rail system but new track and tunnelling has been provided in places to change the route of the old railways. This has allowed a higher standard of public transport service to be operated as the potential for segregation from the rest of British Rail system was available in planning the new metro.'

In Europe where regulations are different, it has been possible to develop street tramways into what are called 'pre-metro' systems with substantial segregation from other street traffic in most cases by the construction of subways in central and other congested areas.

No such proposals have been envisaged in the West Midlands other than a study of a Rapid Transit alternative to the Cross-City line and consideration of a rapid transit system along the Hagley Road corridor. The decision was taken some years ago to use the existing rail network. This was despite the drawbacks of shared track with other services and the fact that the location of stations was governed in many cases by historical sites rather than present day requirements. This also meant that the timetabling of local trains could not always be on a strictly regular pattern which is the ideal in the urban situation.

Major schemes such as a new Metro system need long term commitment covering financial investment and support together with the appropriate land use and transportation policies. Such schemes are, therefore, only possible if they form part of the county's Structure Plan proposals.

A FALSE START

In fact the Passenger Transport Authority and the County Council had already started looking at the possibilities of alternative transport strategies with the formation of the Joint Transportation Planning Unit formed in 1980. The following year as part of this review the unit started a study of light rapid transit. The objects of this study were identified in the West Midlands Structure Plan Review of 1983 as being:

◇ Support and catalyst for economic regeneration by attracting economic development, and by demonstrating a commitment by the County Council to give confidence to the area.
◇ An improved public transport system. Rapid transit could help to reverse the decline in non-car users, and attract people who travel by car. A public transport system based entirely on conventional bus and rail services has limited scope for achieving this aim.
◇ Increased efficiency. Following the full introduction of one-man operated buses further major gains in productivity can now only be achieved by large-scale capital investment.
◇ Energy conservation. By reducing dependence on the private car rapid transit can help reduce energy consumption.
◇ Improved access to central areas. Congestion problems are generally concentrated on approaches to central areas, especially Birmingham City Centre. Rapid transit could be the most appropriate means of increasing public transport's share of the market for trips to the centre of the conurbation and could also improve penetration of the central area by public transport.
◇ Improved environment. Reduced volumes of traffic would bring environmental benefits. Rapid transit could also do a great deal to improve the environment in Birmingham City Centre for shopping and commercial activity, perhaps in association with pedestrianisation schemes.

In June 1984 the final report was presented to the WMCC and WMPTE and recommended an initial network of four corridors radiating from the city centre:

◇ Sutton Coldfield, using the railway alignment to Aston and then via disused land and highway alignments to Gosta Green and the city centre.
◇ Kingstanding (with a branch to Great Barr) using highway alignments and

entering a tunnel at the city centre.
- ✧ Chelmsley Wood, again using highway alignments.
- ✧ West Bromwich. This would use a mixture of highway and railway alignments with through road traffic diverted on to a new by-pass that would use railway land.

In January 1985 the WMCC decided that the first work would be the Chelmsley Wood route, actually going as far as the Firs estate at Hodge Hill.

The corridor selected had never had its arterial roads upgraded in the same way as other ones and there were no former tram central reservations. The result was that 238 separate items of property, much of it housing, were needed to provide a segregated alignment. In the next few months the public local to the scheme, led by a residents' organisation called SMART (Solid Majority Against Rapid Transit) protested against the scheme and persuaded the City Council not to support the scheme. Ultimately the WMCC, which was itself facing extinction, decided not to go ahead with the scheme and the whole concept of rapid transit was put on hold pending local government reform.

A NEW DAWN

However it was not long before politicians in the Black Country were angling for rapid transit and the idea was soon back on the burner. In September 1987, as part of a public awareness scheme that had been going on for some time, the concept of rapid transit under the 'Midland Metro' branding was launched, initially without a route! On this subject there was some dispute between Birmingham and the Black Country but, bearing in mind the problems that had occurred two years before, most players were willing to accept a line that would be simple and not controversial to build. By the time of the launch it was an open secret that the first line was likely to be between Wolverhampton and Birmingham but it was not until 16th February 1988 that the Passenger Transport Authority formally announced this. There would be a choice of three entries into Wolverhampton including street running, the alignment ultimately selected. Things seemed to be going well and no one had any idea that it would be ten years before the first tram arrived.

Under the requirements then needed a Bill to authorise the construction of the line was put before Parliament in November 1988 and proceeded quickly through the various stages, becoming an Act of Parliament a year later. Application for funding was made in April 1990 and thus began a period of frustrating waiting. Not only did the project suffer from a lack of funding but the Government started changing the rules demanding that some private capital should be injected into the scheme.

In October 1991 the Government gave a grant of £1.5m to the PTA, now named Centro, to enable study of the conditions of the ground and structures. Centro were also to plan the project management and examine ways of attracting private finance. Later that month Centro published notice in the official journal of the EC inviting interested parties to apply for a pack that would give them what information they needed to apply to prequalify as a tenderer for line 1, as the project was now known. Four consortia were ultimately applied and finally the project was awarded to Centram, basically consisting of Ansaldo Trasporti and Taylor Woodrow Construction. Even this did not go well with Taylor Woodrow pulling out leaving Ansaldo to recruit another partner and on the 30th October 1993 they announced that John Laing had been taken on board. Just over a year later the Government announced the financing of the scheme subject to extra finance being raised or the costs being cut. There followed a further 6 months of negotiations before Centro managed to persuade the Government that the £143m cost should be split as follows:

	£
UK Government grant and credit approval	80m
European Regional Development Fund	31m
Centro	17m
Altram	10m
Birmingham, Wolverhampton and Sandwell Councils along with the Black Country Development Corporation	4m
Sale of surplus properties	1m

The original cost of £145m had been reduced to £143m by cutting out three stops and having smaller trams.

And so it was that on 3rd August 1995 members of the press, public and local councils met at the Hawthorns railway station to see Rob Donald of Centro, David Blair of John Laing and Giovanni Iacovelli and Decio Lordi of Ansaldo sign an agreement for the construction and operation of line 1 of Midland Metro.

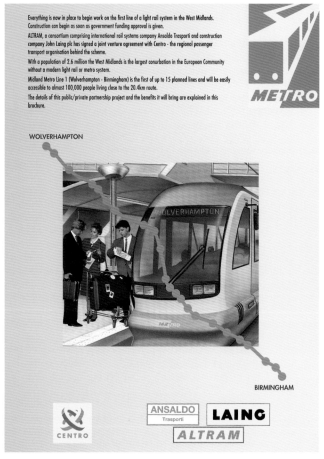

Everything is now in place to begin work on the first line of a light rail system in the West Midlands. Construction can begin as soon as government funding approval is given.

ALTRAM, a consortium comprising international rail systems company Ansaldo Trasporti and construction company John Laing plc has signed a joint venture agreement with Centro - the regional passenger transport organisation behind the scheme.

With a population of 2.6 million the West Midlands is the largest conurbation in the European Community without a modern light rail or metro system.

Midland Metro Line 1 (Wolverhampton - Birmingham) is the first of up to 15 planned lines and will be easily accessible to almost 100,000 people living close to the 20.4km route.

The details of this public/private partnership project and the benefits it will bring are explained in this brochure.

Cover of brochure issued in 1995 giving details of the building and benefits of Metro Line 1.

THE CONSTRUCTION PERIOD

Construction of the 20.4km line commenced on 13th November 1995 when PTA Chairman Richard Worrall and Transport Secretary Sir George Young carried out a groundbreaking ceremony at the site of West Bromwich station, picked because of its easy access. In fact little physical evidence of construction apart from the clearance of 23 years of vegetation growth and the construction of the depot appeared during the first 12 months. In November 1996 an 11 ton 15m long vehicle mock-up arrived and was displayed initially at Wednesbury but later at other sites where the public and more specialist groups were able to evaluate the design.

At about the same time tracklaying commenced, being undertaken by GrantRail, an Anglo-Dutch company. Track was made up into 18 metre lengths at Wednesbury and then 12 lengths were loaded on to flat wagons before being pushed by one of the two Ruston Hornsby diesels to the railhead. Here a Swedish owned Ameca track laying machine would pick up a section of track and position it on the ballast until all sections were unloaded. Alltrack then welded the sections of track together before GrantRail returned to tamp them. Where stops occurred the track was pre-laid on concrete and then coloured blocks were inserted between the rails and platforms to make a paved area.

Despite using the former Great Western Railway alignment there were some major civil engineering works. Between Winson Green and Handsworth, Booth Street the consortia were required to build a viaduct over the access to Queens Head sidings, until recently used by Blue Circle Cement and retained for strategic reasons. This 300m long structure has a ruling gradient of 1-in-30 from the Birmingham end and 1-in-60 from the Wolverhampton side.

The wishbone bridge at Middlecross, Wolverhampton.

The operations and maintenance site is at Wednesbury where it can service both line 1 and any extension to Dudley or Walsall. There are three covered tracks for undertaking maintenance work but rolling stock is normally stored outside. Above this facility the control centre is situated and from here watch is kept through CCTVs on the system. Sanding and washing plants are also in existence but it was not until the summer of 2001 that a wheel lathe was provided and the lack of this facility caused considerable operational problems during the first two years of operation.

At Priestfield the line leaves the railway track bed and runs for 1.3km on a highway-based alignment to the terminus at Wolverhampton St Georges. Track on this section was laid by hand where 18 metre long lengths of rail, pre-encapsulated in insulation material, were bolted to the concrete track bed before being infilled with concrete. On sections shared with other traffic a blacktop finish gives a neat look. Just before the Wolverhampton terminus the line crosses the ring road on the level at the site of a sunken island known as Middlecross. To cross this area and to provide a gateway to Wolverhampton a 60m long flood-lit split-spine girder bridge was built in the year ended July 1997.

The summer of 1997 also saw the commencement of erecting the overhead. Concrete bases had already been installed along the line and so it was a simple exercise to bolt down the poles. For the most part the double contact overhead wire is suspended from crossarms mounted on poles situated at each side of the track. But there are exceptions to this:

◇ Where the line parallels the Jewellery Line railway shortage of space led to the use of crossarms capable of spanning both tracks;
◇ Where street track is used span wiring from poles also used as lighting standards, and
◇ The final approach to Wolverhampton terminus is laid on central reservation and uses poles mounted centrally between the tracks.

The overhead line is fed from substations situated at Snow Hill, near Benson Road, Black Lake, Wednesbury Depot, near Priestfield and at Wolverhampton.

Tram 03 in the workshop at Wednesbury depot.

THE VEHICLES

The contract required the provision of 15 vehicles but the consortium felt that this was not enough and provided one vehicle itself. Designated type T69, the vehicles were built by Firema at their Caserta factory. A strike there at the time of construction was responsible for delaying the opening of the system.

The three section bi-directional trams are 24.36 metres long and 2.6 metres wide with access through three side doors. For approximately 60% of the vehicle length a low floor is provided, normally being 350mm above rail level but dropping to 335mm at the sills and rising to 380mm above the articulation. At the end of the low floor sections steps lead to seating areas and the driver's cab which is 850mm above rail height. The bodyshells are constructed from an aluminium alloy.

There are two powered bogies, which gives the trams a B+2+B wheel arrangement, each with steel welded frames, resilient wheels, suspension consisting of a primary system using rubber springs and a secondary system with air cushioning and a 210 kW motor. Each motor is longitudinally mounted.

The 'vital statistics' of the trams are:

Tare weight	38 tonnes
Minimum horizontal curve	25 metres
Minimum vertical curve	250 metres
Maximum gradient	62.5 %
Line voltage	750 V dc
Auxiliary voltage	24 V dc
Maximum speed	75km/h
Acceleration	1.0 m/s^2
Service braking	1.0 m/s^2

Normally electrodynamic (regenerative and/or rheostatic type) assisted at low speed by an electro hydraulic friction brake.

Emergency braking (track brakes)	2.5 m/s^2
Seating	56

Four seats are tip-up type in bays otherwise used for wheelchairs, pushchairs etc.

Standing	100

The exterior colour scheme of the vehicles was designed by Ray Stenning and comprises a red front and roof lining, a purple body and coupler cover, grey sills, yellow doors and green lining. Inside the body is grey and seating patterned blue. Grabrails are yellow and the door open buttons green.

The cars do have couplers hidden under their front dash but coupled unit operation is something that has only been tried during testing. If, or when, additional capacity is needed then a longer centre section can be inserted and this accounts for the three doors per side layout. Power is collected from the overhead line by a single armed pantograph fitted to the vehicle at the Wolverhampton end.

For various reasons the trams have not performed well and perhaps there was some portent of this when tram 13 was hit by lightning twice just before and after the opening of the line! Quite a few modifications were needed before the Health & Safety Executive would allow operation to commence. The failure to provide a wheel lathe initially caused serious problems with the small trailing wheels fitted under the articulation, which resulted in reduced running speed over crossovers. It seems unlikely that these vehicles will be capable of operating on some of the grades planned for the city centre extension.

Car 16 leaves the Ettingshall Road on its way to Wolverhampton.

Above **An elevated view of trams 07 and 13. Tram 13 has the distinction of having been struck by lightning on two separate occasions.**

Left **Inside a Midland Metro tram.**

OPERATION

The late delivery of the trams meant that the opening of the system was seriously delayed and consideration was given to opening the line in two sections. However Altram had received enough trams by May 1999 to operate a 10-minute service. On Sunday May 23rd an open day was held for those who had been involved in the project and this was followed the following week by the public opening of the system.

The official opening took place on the 30th May and after various speeches the first tram, No. 7, was driven by Angela Trufitt from Snow Hill to Wolverhampton, stopping at West Bromwich and Bilston for further ceremonies. A free service then ran until 6.00pm. At 7.30am the next morning car 10 driven by Balbir Singh set out from Wednesbury Parkway on the first public service to Snow Hill. Unfortunately neither of the ticket machines at that stop were working, something that was to be a regular occurrence over the next two years.

The original idea was to operate a 6-minute peak and 10-minute off-peak service but reliability problems have meant that this has rarely been reached. Despite a variety of locations on the destination displays, apart from returns to the depot, there is only one return service, that from Birmingham Snow Hill to Wolverhampton. As the service is operated by Travel West Midlands through its operating section Travel Midland Metro it has been possible to co-ordinate many local bus services and these carry an 'M' prefix to their route number. Travel West Midlands is a National Express subsidiary as is Central Trains, the local rail operator, and so there has been the ability to co-ordinate ticketing between local rail and the metro. The one rail service that is not operated by Centro yet connects with the metro is the Chiltern Line service to London, originally from Snow Hill but now extended into the Black Country. However this is owned by John Laing plc and so again there is ticketing co-ordination.

Co-ordination with private transport is also provided. Park & ride facilities already existed at the Hawthorns station but three further sites were opened in late 2000 at Priestfield, Wednesbury Parkway and Black Lake. CCTV security is provided at these locations.

As with most light rail systems physical signalling is kept to a minimum and reliance is placed on radio contact with the control centre. Apart from a short single track section through Snow Hill station there is double track all the way and most operation is 'on sight' apart from at crossovers where illuminated route indicators are provided. Signals do exist at some locations, being used on the single track section and co-ordinated with traffic lights where necessary, i.e. at Black Lake, where there is a level crossing, and at Wolverhampton. These are traditional tram signals (if you have been following tram development over the last 40 years) having 5 vertical and horizontal white lights. When a horizontal bar is shown then the tram should wait but it can proceed when a vertical bar is shown.

Security on the system is provided by a detachment of British Transport Police based at the Operations and Maintenance centre. The centre also has visual contact with each stop through CCTV and waiting passengers can speak to control through a two-way public address system. Initially two ticket machines were provided at each halt but despite the above security they suffered from vandalism and were also extremely unreliable. Following a visit to another National Express operated tramway system, Swanson Trams in Melbourne (Australia), it was decided that conductors would be provided and these have now replaced most machines.

Car 12 pauses at The Hawthorns, West Bromwich, where interchange is made with Central Trains services.

There is considerable flexibility in the work of the staff. Even those working in the office are required to be able to drive trams, and keep up to date with this. Drivers also do revenue protection jobs and some minor repair work.

In the first year of operation the metro carried 5 million passengers. This increased by 25% the following year and is continuing to grow at a slower rate. Whilst not yet producing an operating profit the line carried 171% of the passengers carried per mile on the local heavy rail system.

A view at Priestfield, where the original railway alignment continued straight under the A41, which car 08 has just left.

THE FUTURE

The line was always planned to be part of a much larger network and its termini were temporary locations. Centro did get powers for further extensions and routes which would have taken the northern end around Wolverhampton city centre and then to Walsall via Wednesfield and Willenhall. At Walsall the line would have turned south, travelling via Darlaston, Wednesbury and Dudley to Brierley Hill. At the Birmingham end an underground extension would have linked the original line to another one starting at Five Ways Edgbaston and running under the city centre to Aston University. From there the line would have gone on surface via Aston, the Bromford Estate and Chelmsley Wood to the National Exhibition Centre and Birmingham Airport. A branch would have served the Castle Vale Estate. However it was made plain to Centro that these lines were not likely to meet the Government's required levels of return and were abandoned.

A number of 'bite-sized chunks' were identified and two of these have been taken forward. A branch from line 1 at Wednesbury will use the former South Staffordshire and Oxford, Worcester & Wolverhampton Railways to go to Dudley, where a new alignment will take it through the town centre, and on to Brierley Hill where a new alignment will enable it to serve the Merry Hill shopping centre who are willing to invest some £25m in this project.

At the Birmingham end the line will leave the present alignment just before Snow Hill and go on-street through the city centre, serving New Street station and then out along Broad Street to Five Ways. An outline business case for these two projects was accepted by the Government in December 2000 and application for a Transport & Public Works Act Order followed.

Following on from Manchester's successful bid for network funding and a much more positive approach to light rail by the Government, Centro appointed Steer Davies Gleave to examine other corridors for possible light rail operation. In July 2001 Centro decided on the following schemes for development work:

- ◇ Five Ways along the Hagley Road to Quinton or Halesowen. There could be two spurs to Oldbury and Bartley Green.
- ◇ Birmingham city centre to the NEC/airport via the A45 corridor.
- ◇ Walsall to Wolverhampton.
- ◇ Great Barr or Kingstanding through the city centre to Bournbrook or Selly Oak.

In October 2001 the West Midlands Area Multi-modal Study Steering Group produced the Final Report. This called for a number of transport improvements and claimed that they were all complementary and therefore it was necessary to make sure that all proposals should be implemented.

The following light rail routes were proposed over the next 20 years:

Within 10 years

- ◇ Birmingham–Quinton–Halesowen.
- ◇ Birmingham–Sheldon–Birmingham Airport–Chelmsey Wood
- ◇ Walsall–Wolverhampton.

Within 10 to 20 years

- ◇ Birmingham–Chelmsey Wood
- ◇ Birmingham–Northfield
- ◇ A branch off the Quinton line to Bartley Green
- ◇ Walsall–Wednesbury

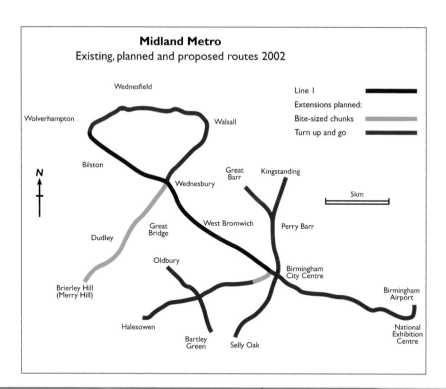

Midland Metro
Existing, planned and proposed routes 2002

Wednesfield

Wolverhampton

Walsall

Bilston

Great Barr

Kingstanding

Wednesbury

West Bromwich

Great Barr

Perry Barr

Dudley

Great Bridge

Oldbury

Birmingham City Centre

Brierley Hill (Merry Hill)

Birmingham Airport

Halesowen

Bartley Green

Selly Oak

National Exhibition Centre

Line I

Extensions planned:

Bite-sized chunks

Turn up and go

N

5km

NOTTINGHAM EXPRESS TRANSIT

The city of Nottingham, population 275,000, is the regional centre for the East Midlands, and after a period of borough status within Nottinghamshire, is once again a unitary authority. However its boundaries do not embrace the whole conurbation, particularly to the south. Here the River Trent, 2km from the city centre, is the boundary with the urban district of West Bridgford. Greater Nottingham counts some 500,000 residents. City and County have therefore always had to work together in matters affecting traffic and transportation, which are not governed by local authority boundaries.

The city first hit the headlines in the transportation sense in the 1970s, when it made a bold attempt to tackle increasing traffic congestion by abandoning road building in favour of the 'zone and collar' scheme. This used traffic signal restrictions to control access to the central area, while priority bus lanes and a fleet of express coaches offered motorists a way of avoiding the queues. However this was unsuccessful in winning over the public, and political pressure caused the scheme to be dismantled.

FIRST THOUGHTS ABOUT LIGHT RAIL

Traffic congestion has continued to grow, and in 1989 the City Council, County Council and Nottingham Development Enterprise (a private-public partnership) jointly commissioned a team of consultants to carry out a feasibility study into a light rail system for Greater Nottingham. Different routes were examined and a corridor between the Midland railway station (south of the city centre) and the north-west suburb of Hucknall was found to offer the best potential for rapid transit.

The County Council was already working on proposals to re-open the closed railway line from Nottingham to Mansfield and Worksop. This project, which came to fruition as the Robin Hood Line, included stations at Hucknall, Bulwell and Basford, providing suburban service to Nottingham Midland station. It was seen that light rail transit could increase the catchment area of conventional rail by providing additional intermediate stations (with interchange at the heavy rail stations for rail network passengers), plus a direct route to the city centre using street track. Light rail could also provide for park-and-ride traffic from the M1 motorway by building a branch west from Old Basford to the site of the former Babbington colliery (now Phoenix Park).

Options for reaching Hucknall alongside the two-track rail alignment included widening to four tracks, some single track at pinch points, and track sharing. The latter, pioneered by Nottingham's German twin city, Karlsruhe, needs to be achieved in a way that satisfies the Railway Inspectorate that a collision between rolling stock with different buffet strengths is impossible. Since 1989 a number of studies have been carried out and technical solutions devised to satisfy this requirement (as met by the Tyne & Wear Metro's extension to Sunderland), but in 1990 there was a good deal of scepticism as to whether it could be achieved. In the event the solution adopted by the consortium selected to build, operate and maintain the line involves alignment sharing, but not track sharing. This decision was made not on safety grounds, but for pragmatic and financial risk reasons.

A detailed study examined route options through the city centre. An obvious alignment was the closed Great Central Railway track bed (disused since 1966) north from the (Midland) railway station through the tunnels either side of the former Victoria station to Mansfield Road, turning west past the Forest recreational area to Hyson Green and a connection with the Robin Hood Line at Wilkinson Street. However the construction of the Victoria Centre, a large shopping complex, on the site of the GC station had blocked the alignment, and tunnelling underneath would have increased the scheme cost by many millions as well as creating long walking routes for passengers.

A street alignment coming off the GC viaduct at Middle Hill and running along Fletcher Gate to Victoria Street, Old Market Square, the Theatre Royal and the Trent University to reach the Forest was selected therefore. This produced some interesting problems to resolve in terms of curvature and gradients, but proved to be within the capabilities of a modern tramway. At that stage the 14-km scheme was costed at about £68 million (1990 prices), with a prediction of about 15,000 passenger journeys per day.

Public consultation showed support for the street-running option and the concept was endorsed by the Greater Nottingham Strategic Transport Study. Consultants were appointed to carry out detailed design work in readiness for the submission of a private Bill to Parliament in November 1991, to obtain the legal authority for the project. At the same time an application for Government funding was prepared. The consortium of promoters (City Council, County Council and Nottingham Development Enterprise) formed Greater Nottingham Rapid Transit Ltd (GNRT) as a joint venture company, and successfully secured private sector contributions towards the development work, from local companies such as Boots and East Midlands Electricity, as well as £500,000 from the European Regional Development Fund.

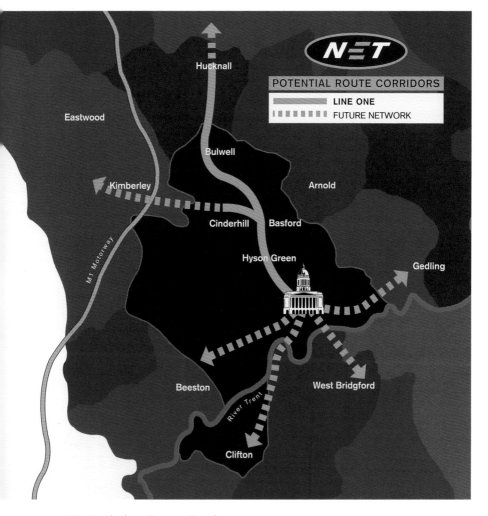

THE PARLIAMENTARY PROCESS

The Greater Nottingham Rapid Transit Bill was examined in Parliamentary committee so that the arguments of objectors could be considered, and finally received Royal Assent in July 1994. At that stage it was hoped that the results of tendering for the design, construction and operation of the project would be available in time to secure a commitment of government funding in 1996. Construction was estimated to take two years.

In 1996 the Arrow Consortium, formed by ABB/AEG (electrical and mechanical engineering), Tarmac (civil engineering), Transdev (project management and operations) and Nottingham City Transport (operating company) was appointed by GNRT to become the project development group, and after formal tendering Arrow was successful in September 1997 in being selected to implement the project as Nottingham Express Transit (NET), under a 30-year franchise. Arrow proposed to supply 15 ABB 'Eurotrams' to work the line, a 100% low-floor articulated design developed for the French city of Strasbourg and built in the UK (initially at York, but later at Derby).

Ironically the election of a Labour government in 1997 was the start of a period of some frustration, as Transport Secretary John Prescott expressed the view that 'trams were too expensive' and 'better buses could do the job just as well', although soon conceding that 'trams have a part to play'. These mixed messages continued for two years, and delayed any announcement of funding for Nottingham. Behind the scenes the promoters were still hard at work, with the Department of the Environment, Transport and the Regions (DETR) and the Treasury insisting that the only way the scheme could go ahead was through the Private Finance Initiative (PFI), transferring the initial funding commitment and revenue risk to the private sector in return for a public financing stream over the period of the franchise.

Finally on 3rd December 1998 the Minister of Transport, John Reid, announced that the Government would provide £167 million to Nottingham City Council to fund its side of the PFI project. This was the Net Present Value of the revenue stream over the 30-year concession period, equivalent to about £16 million/year in local government revenue support. This announcement was just the start of another period of delay, as the financial implications of what was on offer were discussed between the promoters and the Arrow consortium. It became apparent that government grant would lead to a shortfall of £26 million by 2030, requiring the local authorities to contribute £1 million/year above the grant limit. Additionally construction cost increases of £11.6 million had been identified, which would need to be met from city and county sources in 2000–2002. Eventually these figures were agreed at £27.5 million over 31 years, plus £5.6 million during the construction period. The concession was lengthened from 30 to 31 years after it was acknowledged that the construction period would be 42 months rather than 36.

The final go-ahead came on 3rd April 2000, although as early as February the contractors had started to build the project offices on a corner of land adjacent to the new line at the Forest. Road cones started to appear on the street sections from 4th June, and work to divert services commenced on 12th June. Work started on demolishing the Great Central viaduct at Middle Hill to permit the future tramway to make the transition from its own right-of-way to the street (and replace the remainder of the old brick viaduct with a concrete structure).

CONSTRUCTION PROGRAMME

The project plan saw work on utility diversion on the 5-km of street track completed by early 2002, permitting the track bed construction to be finished by August 2002. Major work on the Robin Hood Line was completed by the end of 2001. The first rails were laid in October 2001, and tracklaying and erection of the overhead will run until November 2002, by which time the first tram should have arrived, permitting trial running and then driver training from January to October 2003. Start of public service is scheduled for November 2003.

The passage of time has seen some changes in the names of the participants in the Arrow consortium, though not its make-up. Transdev has taken an 18.5% stake in the municipally-owned Nottingham City Transport. Tarmac Construction has become Carillion, and ADtranz is now part of Bombardier Transportation. Even before the latter move, a fundamental decision had been made about rolling stock. The Eurotram design's power-to-weight ratio, and door-cycling time had proved inadequate to maintain the timetable written in to the contract, and instead the Incentro design (another ADtranz product) was substituted. Incentro is a 33-metre long, 2.4-metre wide, double-ended tram with five body sections and three wheelsets, six double doors each side and a 100% low-floor interior. Each of the 15 trams will have 62 seats and space for up to 138 standing passengers. Maximum design speed will be 80km/h. The first batch to be built started running in the French city of Nantes in autumn 2000, and like Nantes the Nottingham system will be standard gauge (1435mm).

THE ROUTE

NET starts from an elevated station across Station Street (but connected by footbridge) from the Midland railway station and runs north to a new stop proposed to serve the expansion of the adjacent Broad Marsh shopping centre. It then switches to the street (Fletcher Gate), with a stop at the north end serving the Lace Market district. The tight turn (an 18-m radius curve) west into Victoria Street follows, taking the trams along the south side of the Council House to the important city centre stop Old Market Square.

From here the tramway turns north again along Market Street to cross Upper Parliament Street to serve the Royal Centre, continuing along Goldsmith Street to Trent University. Waverley Street has a stop for the High School for Boys, before the line runs along the west side of The Forest to a stop of the same name, which in addition to being a 990-space park-and-ride, will serve the annual Goose Fair ground.

Through Hyson Green the northbound and southbound tracks split, with the former in Noel Street and the latter in Radford Road, each with two stops. Northbound there is also a stop at Shipstone Street, before the tracks come together again in Wilkinson Street, the last stop on the street section (serving an 800-space park-and-ride). The depot is here. A curving embankment takes the NET tracks down to the west side of the Robin Hood rail line, where there is room for four tracks (two tram, two train) through Basford and north to Highbury Vale, the junction for the short branch to Cinderhill and Phoenix Park (675 park-and-ride spaces).

North of Highbury Vale both tram and train come down to single track to squeeze through the pinch point of Bulwell interchange. From here there are parallel single tracks for trams and trains with a passing loop at Moor Bridge park-and-ride (118 spaces). The tramway terminates in a stub terminus at Hucknall beside the Railtrack station, and another park-and-ride (457 spaces).

The total of 3,040 park-and-ride spaces along the line sets it apart from the other new tramway systems built so far in the UK, and makes a significant contribution towards the viability of the project in what may be regarded as a 'small' city. 30,000 passengers a day are now expected to use the trams, taking 2 million car journeys per year off city streets.

At peak periods there will be a tram every six minutes through the city centre, with a 15-minute service to both Hucknall and Phoenix Park, and two trams per hour turning back at Highbury Vale. At quiet hours, including evenings and Sundays, there will be two trams per hour to both Hucknall and Phoenix Park.

With line 1 well underway, the promoters have been studying other corridors for light rail potential in order to achieve the benefits of the 'network effect'. Both City and County councils have carried out studies, which identified routes to Clifton, Beeston and West Bridgford as having the best potential. The City's £855,000 Local Transport Plan bid for 2001/2, accepted by the government, includes funding for work to take the proposals to Transport & Works Act stage in 2002, allowing a full funding bid in 2003. The Arrow consortium, which originally wished to await the results of line 1's operation before committing to expansion, now believes that the climate is much more favourable to new light rail schemes, and is supporting this fast-track approach, which could see a three-route network in use by 2010.

A panorama of Portsmouth Hard showing the tramway emerging past the Dockyard Gate (right), then swinging into the tunnel portal.

SOUTH HAMPSHIRE RAPID TRANSIT
Fareham – Gosport – Portsmouth

The area of south-east Hampshire around Portsmouth is very flat, with Portsdown Hill as a steep backdrop. The many creeks and inlets have been home to the Royal Navy and its supporting industries for centuries. Portsmouth, the densest urban area outside London, first had trams as early as 1865. An intensively worked system on Portsea island gave way to the trolleybus in the mid-1930s.

Two separate tramways served outlying areas, both operated by the Provincial Tramways Company. The line from Fareham to Gosport lasted from 1906 to 1929, and that from Portsmouth/Cosham to Horndean from 1903 to 1935. Ironically, both lines closed just as large-scale housing development was beginning. Fareham–Gosport was also served by a branch railway; this closed to passengers in 1953 leaving Gosport as the largest UK community without a station.

Over the years traffic conditions deteriorated, rendering Provincial's bus services ever more unreliable; the A32 is effectively the only road into Gosport. By the late 1980s it became clear that Gosport was becoming seriously disadvantaged, as its defence-related industries were in a steady decline, and congestion on the 'way out' worsened.

EVOLUTION OF THE LIGHT RAIL PROJECT

The problem of access to/from the Gosport peninsula has been recognised for some time. Road improvements planned in the 1970s never came about, except in the vicinity of Fareham, and these were rapidly swamped with extra traffic. Any road-based solution would very clearly have a severe effect on adjacent properties, and in 1988 the emphasis switched with Hampshire County Council commissioning a study to identify corridors suited to rapid transit in the south of the county. Out of 22 corridors the two shortlisted were Fareham–Gosport and Portsmouth & Southsea–Waterlooville. The former was considered to offer the best potential for light rail, so more detailed studies then took place.

In 1992, there was a major public consultation in which light rail and various guided bus options were offered. The public response of nine per cent (considered good for this type of exercise) gave a 70% vote in favour of the more expensive light rail option. Further local consultations led to changes, so as to minimise any objections. One such example was the avoidance of houses built on the approach to Gosport's old station; street running avoided substantial demolition. In the 1995/96 public consultation, a 92% rate of support gave Hampshire a clear mandate to proceed, so the County unanimously decided to make a Transport & Works Act (TWA) submission. Meanwhile on 1st April 1997 Portsmouth became a Unitary Authority (seceding from Hampshire), and the City Council has co-promoted the project since.

The tunnel under Portsmouth Harbour distinguishes this scheme from others in the UK. It is at once very costly to build, but as an effective monopoly on the route, it should be a moneyspinner. Private sector interest has accordingly been very high from an early stage. The Promoters have themselves stimulated this interest by fleshing out many details (the number of trams needed, body width, etc), so as to quantify risks and revenue. The economic and social case will be explored in more detail later.

THE ROUTE

The tramway, 14.3km in length with 16 stops, will start at Fareham's bus station in the commercial centre. A single-track one-way loop will run on West Street, and back along the north side of Western Way, converging at the traffic-signalled road junction by Fareham station. After stopping on the station forecourt, the line will continue northwards as single-track, and burrow under the railway in a 180 degree curve to emerge facing south on the west side. A new bridge over The Avenue will carry the line on to the old Gosport branch.

The tramway then follows the rail alignment in a dead straight line through Bridgemary and past the depot site at Rowner Road. The existing cycle path on this part of the old trackbed will be moved to one side to make room for the tramway. The line will then skirt round development at Toronto Place, where the old triangular junction leading to Stokes Bay once was, and then cut across Forton Field to join Forton Road. This option, following the former tramway, avoids the new housing on the approach to Gosport's old station. The street tramway continues along Mumby Road, North and South Cross Street and South Street. Here it offers connections at the Esplanade bus interchange by the present ferry terminal. At this point it descends into the 1km immersed tube tunnel, described overleaf.

On the Portsmouth side, trams will emerge and stop just to the north of the Harbour station, again offering interchange with other modes. Returning to the streets, the tramway will sweep past the Dockyard entrance to continue along

Queen Street, Edinburgh Road and Stanhope Road. The terminus will be just north of Portsmouth & Southsea station. 70% of the route is segregated and 30% street running.

No park-and-ride facilities are included in the plans; it was felt that the scheme is fully justified simply serving its immediate catchment area, and hopefully by offering excellent interchange with trains and buses. The authorities will keep this issue under review. Planned frequencies are 7½ minutes in the peaks and 15 minutes off-peak.

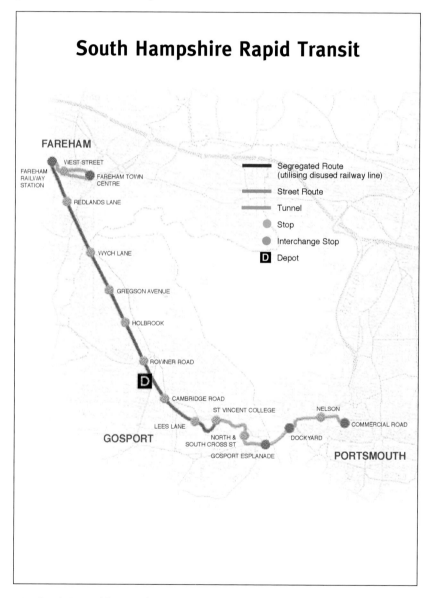

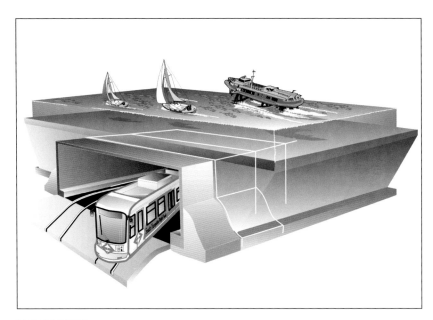

THE TUNNEL

The crossing of Portsmouth Harbour entrance is at once the most expensive element of the project, and the one that underwrites its economic and social justification. A bored tunnel was ruled out as being very expensive and so deep as to give poor interchange at either waterfront; the cut-and-cover option would have caused unacceptable disruption to shipping activity. The choice is therefore the immersed tube.

It is anticipated that a dedicated shuttle will operate through the tunnel for the benefit of cyclists. A tram with no seats, but with racking, will run every 7.5 minutes between service cars. Stub sidings are anticipated at the Gosport Esplanade and Dockyard stops.

At either end will be a 105-metre long portal, taking the line down from the street to beneath sea level. The Portsmouth end portal will be wider, as it will contain the Dockyard stop plus a third stub-end track for the cycle shuttle service. The portals will probably be constructed within a cofferdam.

The tunnel itself will consist of six pre-cast concrete segments totalling 720 metres in length. These may be fabricated off-site and brought to the harbour. The very experienced Dutch consultants did a great deal of detailed work with the harbour authorities and mariners to demonstrate how the shipping lanes will be diverted, so that first one half of the alignment can be dredged, then the other. Once dredged, each segment is floated and sunk into position on the seabed, during an 8-hour overnight closure of the harbour. The three sections on the Gosport side will be the first in place, then the three on the Portsmouth side will go in, culminating in a concreted 'closing joint' between the last two elements. The seabed will then be backfilled to its former level, partly to lock in and protect the tunnel, but also to stop its tendency to float off!

Within the fine detail of this work, mention is made of the option to allow the shared use of the tunnel by kerb-guided electric buses.

THE PUBLIC INQUIRY

In March 1998 the Transport & Works Act application was submitted to the DETR. Prior to this all interested parties (adjoining property owners, other operators, utilities etc) were formally notified of this, and had a 42-day period in which to write to the Secretary of State, either to support or to object to the proposals. In view of the number of objections Mr Prescott called for a Public Inquiry. Due to the complexity of the case, this was not convened until 9th February 1999, the Inspector being Walter Thrush.

In practice, objections could be received right up to the time the Inquiry was sitting, and in the event 454 were received. Many were from elderly people concerned about the disruption and noise caused by construction work, also property devaluation and parking problems. There were at least three lots of pro-forma letters distributed by campaigners in all three communities. Objections from Railtrack and utilities were of a statutory nature, to protect their interests rather than to oppose the scheme outright.

Gosport Borough Council also raised 20 statutory objections; in fact some councillors tried to upset things in the run-up to the Inquiry by forcing a Council vote against the whole project. In the event most of the objections were resolved – indeed around 40 overall were withdrawn before the Inquiry commenced, as a result of dialogue with the light rail project team.

On the supporters' side were various pro-rail organisations. To counter the objections, the local Friends of the Earth branch, the Railway Development Society and Light Rail Transit Association formed the Pro-Metro Alliance. Campaigning and leaflet distribution ultimately boosted the letters of support to over 100.

Once again demonstrating their flexibility, the light rail project team made a last-minute detail change to their plans. Great concern had been expressed at the disruption to road traffic on Newgate Lane just south of Fareham. This crosses the line at-grade, but both are on embankments. It was decided that the tramway could burrow under the road by removing the old railway embankment here.

At the Inquiry, the case for the project was made by barrister Charles George. A total of 14 expert witnesses were called, each presenting evidence on topics such as economic appraisal, engineering, traffic, ecology, property issues and the tunnel. Each could be cross-examined by objectors, or asked for clarification by the Inspector. This process took two days. Following this, any supporter was able to present evidence by prior arrangement. Members of the Pro-Metro Alliance and a disabled lobbyist presented evidence from independent viewpoints.

After this came the objectors. Many of these had settled beforehand; those that remained faced Mr George's razor-sharp intellect, and a formal rebuttal by the co-promotors. The most serious objection was that of the Portsea Harbour Ferry Company, who of course stood to lose their business. They urged a mixed solution, of tram–ferry–tram. The Inquiry closed on 11th March 1999, two weeks earlier than planned.

Following the Inquiry there was a lengthy period of silence in Whitehall. It was rumoured that the Inspector's report had reached the DETR by July 1999, yet nothing certain was heard. When in December the government announced its local transport spending package, the project was excluded. Concerns had been raised that it was too expensive. Nevertheless optimism was maintained by the level of interest from the private sector, and by continuing dialogue between DETR officials and the Light Rail Project team.

A tram emerges from Queen Street, Portsmouth, and passes the Dockyard entrance as it turns on to the Hard.

A view looking across Gosport High Street into South Cross Street. Some buildings will be constructed here to permit double track.

THE ECONOMIC AND SOCIAL CASE

In April 2000 DETR issued new guidelines for major public transport schemes – the New Approach To Appraisal (NATA). When government had previously 'moved the goalposts' light rail tended to suffer as a result: for example, Sheffield Supertram had to be reappraised in the light of bus deregulation. In this instance the criteria seem very much in light rail's favour; Hampshire was determined to be first off the mark in repackaging its case.

Any grant application should now consist of a single Investment Appraisal Document. This should have five main elements: scheme description, problems and objectives (socio-economic), problem mitigation, assessment against Central Government objectives, and against local objectives.

Although one would consider south-east Hampshire to be a relatively affluent area, it does have its problems. On the one hand population density is high, yet on the other, movement is restricted by the coastal geography. Traffic growth in Hampshire is double the national rate; more planned housing and the new Gunwharf shopping complex in Portsmouth will add to this problem. Car ownership rates are however low, and some areas on the tram route contain pockets of high unemployment and deprivation.

Some of these problems may appear unrelated to tram development, but it is evident just what relief the trams would bring, eg by complementing the regeneration of old Defence sites, turning round declining use of public transport, offering a direct cross-harbour journey and relieving the heavily-congested A32 road. Suddenly, the goals of 'social inclusion', and that other government buzz-word 'joined-up transport', are fulfilled magnificently.

Central government objectives come under five main criteria:

✧ Integration (of transport modes, land-use planning, and other 'hot' issues like health, education and creating a more 'inclusive' society).
✧ Safety (of operation, and personal security).
✧ Economy (transport efficiency and business growth).
✧ Environmental impact.
✧ Accessibility (issues of land severance, impact on non-car owners, 'social inclusion').

An Appraisal Summary Table provides a tabulated reference guide to these factors as identified and quantified. These issues are then analysed in much more detail by methods prescribed within the DETR guidelines, including:

Cost/Benefit Analysis
　　　　　　This well-tried tool measures the tangible and less-tangible costs and benefits of a project. The estimated 11.7 million annual trips would generate an impressive operating ratio of 2.4:1. The full economic appraisal, looking at benefits to users and non-users, gives a benefit/cost ratio of c3:1. Here the new criteria now favour trams as the old Section 56 appraisal only considered non-users. In this respect the playing field has levelled out.

TEE-Table　This table analyses the economic efficiency of the transport system, looking at time savings, costs, revenues, subsidies and the benefit/cost ratio. All of this is tabulated so as to illustrate the proposal's overall value for money.

Risk Register　The co-promoters have produced an analysis of risk probabilities for all aspects of construction and operation. This also forms part of the investment appraisal, and will be included in the Outline Business Case.

Deal Testing   Sessions were held with the private sector and three selected consortia have held detailed discussions with the promoters: **Balfour Beatty Consortium** – also including WS Atkins, Transtec, TEC and Volker Stevin; **Harbour Area Rapid Transit** – AMEC, Symonds Group, Bombardier and First Group; **South Hampshire Rapid Transit Alliance** – including McAlpine, Connex, Ove Arup, Posford Duvivier and van Laerge.

These discussions have produced a very positive result: for example, the choice of light rail was upheld, and the capital outlay of £152 million was agreed as realistic.

Appraisal of alternatives   This was rigorously looked into back in 1995 and during the Inquiry. Alternatives included guided bus, a truncated light rail line retaining the ferry, and bus priority measures. None offered the same value for money and performance as light rail; indeed recent government thinking reinforces this view. Low-cost measures such as bus lanes would achieve a very small impact; in any case the A32 has little scope for this. Rail transport has a sense of permanence about it, and people will plan their lives around this.

THE GREEN LIGHT

As 2001 approached, hopes remained high, especially with talk of an impending general election. On 29th March Deputy Prime Minister John Prescott announced that public funding would be forthcoming, even though he had yet to pronounce on the Inquiry – after over two years.

On 8th May came the long-awaited statement – an order under the Transport & Works Act, and planning permission, were to be granted. The supporting evidence was fully endorsed, but the only minor caveat was over park-and-ride. Although this was not viewed as necessary, parking in local roads might need to be controlled. Carriage of cycles on service trams should be left to 'market forces'. The Inspector felt that the ferry company's objection was not sufficiently convincing to overturn the principle of the scheme.

At the time of writing, the Project Team are preparing for the procurement phase. It will take about 18 months to select a consortium who will build and operate the line; construction will last three years, so we should see trams running in Hampshire again in 2006. Eleven trams will be needed to operate the service.

Edinburgh Road, Portsmouth, along which trams could be running within five years.

SOUTH YORKSHIRE SUPERTRAM

During the latter part of the nineteenth and the twentieth century, trams were a new and effective way of transporting people relatively cheaply. However with the introduction of the motor car, cities became more and more congested and in Britain at least, trams had to go. Our European neighbours, with the exception of France, were far more forward looking and developed rather than discarded their systems. In 1960 Sheffield became the last major English city to scrap its Local Authority owned, tram system. During the past few years it is one of the British cities, which has wisely introduced a new light rail tramway, named Supertram. The motor car has become a victim of its own success and congested cities are now nearing total blockage during parts of the day. Along with this, environmental factors have come to the fore and alternative methods of transport have become very important.

HISTORY OF SUPERTRAM DEVELOPMENT

The genesis of the South Yorkshire Supertram lies with a transportation study completed in July 1976 (Sheffield & Rotherham Land Use Transportation Study), which recommended a fixed track segregated system along six corridors in the City of Sheffield. It was expected at that time that the new system would work with and be complemented by the bus system. However political interference put a stop to such benefits. The idea of integration never materialised and, since opening, the tramway has been in direct competition with the multitude of bus companies, that have invaded the streets of the City.

In 1979 the then South Yorkshire County Council (SYCC) as Highway Authority approved in principle the safeguarding of six corridors, and a Joint Transportation Unit comprising officers of SYCC and South Yorkshire Passenger Transport Executive (SYPTE) was established. During 1982–1983 preliminary studies, with emphasis on a line from the Hillsborough area in the north-west to Mosborough in the south-east, examined the characteristics of different modes. The unit investigated both European and American practices and following extensive studies developed plans for a modern, high quality light rail system to ease traffic problems and to aid regeneration of Sheffield. During 1984–1985, technical evaluation reports were produced for this line.

Two significant pieces of legislation took place to affect the scheme. Firstly the Local Government Act abolished the Metropolitan Counties and the 1985 Transport Act brought about de-regulation of local bus services outside London. With the former, SYCC was abolished and its duties as Highway Authority were transferred to Sheffield City Council (SCC), and SYPTE under the 1985 Act was divested of its operating ability. However Supertram survived both.

With an increase in traffic of 16% in Sheffield in the period 1985 to 1989 and a massive 27% decline in bus patronage, journey times were lengthening especially in the City Centre as traffic congestion grew. In the City Centre, parking spaces are at a premium. Peak hour traffic flows block the City's highway system. By providing a car-competitive service, Supertram attracts car users especially commuters. Powered by electricity Supertram is environmentally friendly, with no vehicle exhaust affecting the city atmosphere. Supertram was seen as the most cost-effective mode. Trolleybuses, which were investigated, would not produce the high productivity required.

During this period much of the transportation modelling by MVA Consultants was undertaken, leading to the application to the Department of Transport for a section 56 grant (i.e. Section 56 of the Transport Act 1968) towards the capital cost of the scheme.

In 1989, SYPTE engaged Kennedy Henderson in conjunction with SCC, Department of Design and Building Services (DBS) to produce performance specifications for the design and construction of the tramway infrastructure.

In the same year a project team was formed with the appointment of a Chief Executive and the formation of South Yorkshire Supertram Ltd (SYSL), a wholly owned subsidiary of SYPTE. In addition to SYPTE and SYSL, the project team consisted of Turner & Townsend Project Management Ltd as overall project managers, who engaged Kennedy Henderson to provide light rail engineering design management (E&M) and trackwork inspection services. SCC as Highway Authority was a key player in the project team although not contracted. However DBS Consultancy was contracted to provide highway design, traffic engineering, some structure design and resident engineer supervision for the client. The project was now ready to appoint contractors.

At the time Supertram was being promoted it was necessary to present a Bill to Parliament to seek powers to develop and operate a system of light rail transit and to have certain rights bestowed on its promoters. SYPTE, as promoter, deposited the original Bill in 1985, and this took an extraordinarily long time to be enacted, this not happening until 1988. This Bill was to gain powers to build what was described as Line 1, Middlewood and Stannington in the north-west to Halfway in the south-east via the city centre. Throughout 1986 to 1988 there was considerable consultation with SCC and others in order to seek their support for the Bill. This consultation resulted in a number of modifications (e.g. the Stannington branch being cut back to Malin Bridge for political reasons) and a number of undertakings to protect SCC's position. Also a further Bill was deposited in 1988 for an extension of the system along the Lower Don Valley to serve the then proposed Meadowhall Shopping Centre and to act as a catalyst for the re-development of the old industrial heart of the City. This was described as Line 2. Two further Bills were presented in 1989 and 1990 to gain extra powers.

The total cost of the Supertram project amounted to £240.6 million and by the end of 1990 financial approval was given by the Department of Transport. Unfortunately what had appeared to be a straightforward financing package was somewhat clouded when the Conservative Government stood back from its promise that the scheme would not cost the ratepayers of South Yorkshire 'a penny'. Subsequent financial problems dogged the system and the local newspaper, although it had reported the Minister's words at the time, continued its anti-Supertram stance by continually rubbishing everything to do with it. This is a very strange attitude for any newspaper to take, particularly if Government investment in its area of influence is at stake.

The scheme was financed as follows:

Capital Grant (the then Section 56 Grant from the DoT)	£66.6m
Grant from the European Union	£13.1m
Developer Contributions	£8.0m
Borrowings: 'Non-trading' with debt charges reimbursed	£71.2m
'Trading' to be met from sale of the Franchise Operation,	£81.7m
Total	£240.6m

The privatisation of SYSL on 19th December 1997 accrued £1.5million, which left a substantial deficit, which the local press said would have to be covered by local ratepayers. After discussions with the new Labour Administration's Department of Environment, Transport and the Regions in 1997, the outstanding deficit was converted into a 'Non Trading' grant, which alleviated this problem.

By advertising in the Official European Journal, expressions of interest were invited in September 1988, and a short list of potential contractors and rolling stock manufacturers was drawn up by SYPTE. After careful analysis Balfour Beatty Power Construction Ltd (BB) was awarded the contract for the design and build of the infrastructure and Siemens/Duewag of Düsseldorf for the vehicle supply. Infrastructure costs, including diversions of utilities, were £141m and the trams cost £42m in total.

DESIGN PROCESS

Initially a swept path alignment (SPA) was developed by DBS taking into account the vehicle size and its requirement to traverse minimum horizontal radii of 25 metres and vertical radii of 1.65metres. This SPA was then developed into a Dynamic Kinetic Envelope to model the maximum throw of the vehicle in service.

Emphasis was given to designing Supertram into the existing streetscene. High quality surfaces, structures, stops and street furniture were designed to reflect the premier service to be offered. Special consideration was given to environmentally sensitive areas such as the city centre.

Very importantly the design procedure included consultation with SCC officers and members, and later the general public. Public meetings and exhibitions were held to discuss the concept. As a result of this consultation, the original proposal of taking the tram through the Manor Estate was altered to the route as built along City Road.

In July 1991, SYSL commissioned the Centre for Logistics and Ergonomics at Cranfield Institute to conduct ergonomic studies of the proposed vehicles and tramstops. These studies led to recommending vehicle/platform interface, door design, push button design, handrail positioning, seat design and platform tactile designs etc.

CONSTRUCTION DETAILS

Before construction work could start on the tramway proper, it was necessary to divert the Statutory Undertakers' equipment such as main sewerage, electric cables, gas pipes etc. This had the effect of extending the time the streets of the city were in disarray, which was not very popular with the city's population. Traffic Management schemes were necessary to direct other road users during this stage and tramway construction proper.

Construction of the system took place in eight phases:

Phase 1   Fitzalan Square to Meadowhall (Including South Street Bridge)
Phase 2   South Street Bridge to Spring Lane
Phase 3   Fitzalan Square to University
Phase 4   University to Kelvin
Phase 5   Spring Lane to White Lane and Herdings Park
Phase 6   White Lane to Donetsk Way
Phase 7   Donetsk Way to Halfway
Phase 8   Kelvin to Malin Bridge and Middlewood

The tramway is 29km long and it was necessary to lay some 60km of track bed with approximately 120km of rail and a similar length of contact wire to carry the power supplies. More than 30 new structures had to be built ranging from an Underpass, two 300metre viaducts at Park Square and Norfolk Park, to small retaining walls at various places.

Tram 113 leaving the underpass at University, on the Blue route to Halfway. The tram is in the new livery.

TRAMWAY TRACK

The tramway, 50% of which is segregated from other traffic, features two types of track – tramway track where either pedestrians or road vehicles need to share the right of way and ballasted railway type where there is no such requirement. Large sections of segregated route are ballasted track filled with gravel ballast; others are finished in plain concrete or colour-imprinted concrete in environmentally sensitive areas.

In order to carry out building the street track in the shortest possible time BB used a slip-form paver to produce this concrete base. This was the first time such a machine had been used in tramway construction. Ready mixed concrete, to a specific quality, was delivered by lorry and poured onto a conveyor, feeding a screw, which forced the mix under the machine to produce the concrete bed.

Each track in the highway sits on a concrete bed 2.20 metres wide, with two channels measuring 170 x 165mm for the rails. The grooved rails, SE1–35G, were secured in their channels by a special, solvent free polyurethane adhesive incorporating cork. This compound proved to be prone to de-bonding and unfortunately had low skid resistance for other road users. Therefore after a period the majority was replaced using a similar but better skid resistant material which included bauxite chippings in the mix. These remedial works included surface treatment and white lining to help drivers of other vehicles on the shared sections has taken place.

A third elastomer ALH, also with a high skid resistance value, is to be found on the tramway, and is the preferred material used by the current maintenance contractor – Porterbrook Maintenance Ltd. The reason for using this elastomeric material was to reduce noise and vibration, and to electrically insulate the trams from the surrounding carriageway.

BS-80A flat bottomed rail section, supplied by British Steel Track Products of Workington, fixed to twin block reinforced concrete sleepers with the 'Pandrol' elastic rail fastening system was used on the segregated ballasted track formation. In instances where non-standard track assembly is required (e.g. rail expansion joints, check rail or guardrail etc) timber sleepers are employed.

During construction it was agreed to trial a short section of the experimental LR55 rail section at Alsing Road crossing. This is still in place after seven years use. Recently another experiment has taken place at Fitzalan Square, where a section of pre-coated rail using the ALH system has been installed.

POWER SUPPLY AND OVERHEAD LINE EQUIPMENT

The power supply system consists of twelve 600 kW traction sub-stations approx-imately equi-spaced each of which feeds an electrically common overhead conductor system (OCS) at 750V dc. Each traction sub-station receives a supply from a Yorkshire Electricity ring at 11 kV ac. The OCS is designed for 750V dc working with vehicle operating speeds of up to 80km/h. On the mainline it is usual to employ twin 107mm conductor wires for each direction of travel, although there are a few exceptions. In the depot single conductors are used.

In general the conductor wire is supported by cantilevers attached to poles which are situated either at between or on both sides of the track.

In environmentally sensitive areas such as the City Centre the conductor wires are supported by a head-on arrangement attached by anchorages to nearby build-ings. For maximum environmental and aesthetic benefits, extensive use has been made of lightweight nylon span ropes rather than insulated steel wire. The con-ductor wires are normally between 5 and 6.3 metres above the rail level depending on whether the track is segregated. Over 2300 poles are used.

Gleadless Town End tramstop. Note Section Isolator pole in foreground.

SIGNALLING

All tram movements are under line-of-sight rules, but light rail signalling is provided at road junctions. Two short lengths of single line are controlled by block safety signalling.

The Vehicle Information System (VIS) is a major part of the signalling equipment, and provides the vehicle-to-ground data transmission system. It is in two parts, the ground mounted equipment (Outstation Transmission Units) and the tram-borne equipment, which responds as a tram passes over the Interrogator Loop between the rails. Data transmitted is used for routeing of trams (i.e point changing) and for requesting priority at traffic light controlled road crossings and pedestrian access points. LRT multi-bulb signal heads are used throughout the system.

OPENING OF THE SYSTEM

Before opening any section the Railway Inspectorate inspected the tramway and route training for drivers was instigated.

Supertram opened in stages, (not in construction phase order) commencing on 21st March 1994 when the line from the City Centre (Fitzalan Square) and Meadowhall opened for public service. Later, on 23rd May 1994, HRH the Princess Royal officially opened the Supertram system and was therefore the first Royal to travel on the new Sheffield tram. Prince Charles followed his sister's footsteps later.

Followed by:

Fitzalan Square to Spring Lane	22nd August 1994
Spring Lane to Gleadless Townend	5th December 1994
Fitzalan Square to Cathedral	18th February 1995
Cathedral to Shalesmoor	27th February 1995
Gleadless Townend to Halfway	27th March 1995
Gleadless Townend to Herdings Park	3rd April 1995

Finally came the stretch from Shalesmoor to Malin Bridge and Middlewood, opened on 23rd October 1995. Prior to this, the opportunity was taken to publicise the imminent opening of the final stage, by hiring an original Sheffield horse tram, number 15 of 1873, from the National Tramway Museum which was paraded alongside a new Supertram vehicle at the Cathedral.

There are three colour-coded routes. As a point of history, Sheffield has never had tram route numbers. The original system just showed the terminal point on the screen, whilst Supertram uses colour coding as well.

OPERATION

Initially the service trams stopped at every stop, but very quickly it was realised that this was delaying the service. Now the tramway operates a request only service. Passengers wishing to alight must press a button to advise the driver that they wish to do so. On stopping the driver will enable the doors to open, but they will not do so until the passenger again presses the button. The driver then closes the doors and disables them before the tram can move.

There are 48 tramstops in total, all, with the exception of the terminal points and Netherthorpe Road, being two-side platform design. The terminal points (except Meadowhall Interchange) understandably are single platform, whilst Netherthorpe Road and Meadowhall Interchange are island platforms with two faces. Each platform has information cases with tram service times, fares and general information. No CCTV nor public address is available. Every platform has tactile paving both longitudinal and at right angles to the tram. These help guide those passengers with sight disabilities to find the doors of the vehicles. The driver lines his sight up to painted marks on the platform to be sure the doors will be in line.

A passenger in a motorised chair entering a tram at Fitzalan Square.

The Blue Route operates from Halfway terminus via Crystal Peaks Shopping Centre, Gleadless Townend, Norfolk Park, close to Sheffield United football ground, Sheffield Station (also serving Sheffield Hallam University) through the City Centre central shopping and business areas, Cathedral and University of Sheffield, before travelling to Hillsborough and terminating at Malin Bridge.

The Yellow Route operates from Middlewood, passes Sheffield Wednesday football ground at Hillsborough, serves the large important suburban shopping centre before joining the Blue Route at Hillsborough Corner and traverses the same route to the City Centre. After Fitzalan Square it diverges from the Blue Route at Park Square Delta Junction, and serves the Lower Don Valley with its remaining steel factories. It also serves the relatively new sporting and leisure facilities of the Don Valley International Stadium and Sheffield Arena, and a very new leisure complex with a new tramstop called 'Valley Centertainment', before Meadowhall Retail Park and terminating at Meadowhall Shopping Centre.

The Purple Route operates from Herdings Park, which is a short distance from Gleadless Townend at which point it joins the Blue Route and runs the same path to the Cathedral, where it reverses and operates as the Yellow Route to Meadowhall, described above.

Although no Park & Ride sites were provided in the original build of Supertram, SYPTE has retrospectively built three sites – at Halfway Terminus, Middlewood Terminus and Nunnery Square. A further site was already in use for bus and rail passengers at Meadowhall Interchange and the use of this site increased after the tram became operational so that the PTE doubled its size. A non-PTE site is also used at The Valley Centertainment Leisure Park. The PTE-operated sites (with the exception of Meadowhall which is free) have a charge of £3 Daily which includes a day's tram pass, whilst the non-PTE site is also free. Motorists using these sites are benefiting from using the very popular tram for their journeys into the city and this in turn cuts the number of motor vehicles in the city centre during the day.

During the day (Monday to Saturday) a 10-minute frequency is provided on the Blue and Yellow routes and 30 minute frequency on the Purple route. Early morning and after 19.00 a 20-minute frequency is provided on the Blue and Yellow routes whilst the Purple route increases to 20 minute on the south-east leg only. This is so that a 10-minute service can be provided to Gleadless Townend. This pattern of service means Hillsborough to the City Centre has a 5-minute service during the day and a 10-minute service at other times. The service hours are 06.00 to 24.00. Sunday service sees a 20-minute pattern on all routes.

There are 82 drivers, 77 conductors, 11 control room and 6 administration staff to keep the wheels rolling. Two signing-on points are provided.

Sheffield as a City has moved away from its traditional heavy steel industry to a service/light engineering base. This has brought with it a steep drop in the numbers employed and a severe drop in its economic status. However Supertram is seen as one way of improving this state of affairs and it is noticeable how often the tram is featured in developer's advertisements and also Estate Agent information. Supertram has improved accessibility into the Lower Don Valley and helped develop commercial activity.

The City Council and others are very keen on exploiting the benefits of the Supertram system, and have produced literature outlining Development Opportunities along the Supertram Corridors. Other firms are known to have taken into account the presence of Supertram in their considerations of moving to the City.

FARES/REVENUE PROTECTION

It was originally intended that all revenue collection would take place off the tram, ticket sales being from on-stop machines with validation machines alongside. This was complemented by sales of packets of tickets from selected retail outlets (newsagents, tobacconists, PTE shops etc) at discounted rates.

Unfortunately due to very high levels of vandalism and fare evasion (It seems that the British are not very honest in such circumstances), on-tram roving conductors equipped with Wayfarer ticket machines were virtually forced onto the tramway, firstly as an experiment from Halfway to Gleadless Townend only. After this successful experiment Halfway/Herdings Park to Sheffield Station converted to conductor operation on 6th May 1996, with the remainder of the system on 17th June 1996. This has proved exceptionally beneficial in terms of reducing fare evasion, cutting vandalism, providing a high level of personal security for passengers and the most often quoted benefit – people prefer to deal with another person not a faceless machine. Single, return, daily and weekly tickets are sold in this way. However sometimes it is very difficult for one roving conductor to deal with the crowds on board and therefore at peak times and other special circumstances, such as sporting events, the tram conductor has help from a specially employed staff. It is possible therefore to see two conductors on board at these times. Stagecoach management believes this is still cost-effective, and although it plans to install on-stop machines at certain City Centre stops, the on-tram conductor is and will remain a very important asset to the operating company.

PATRONAGE

Understandably patronage takes time to develop on any new system which has to operate in conditions as imposed in British provincial cities. Competitors almost inevitably react by trying to price themselves into the market and stop the newcomer in its 'tracks'. This happened in Sheffield but due to the tram's superior image, better riding quality and overall ambience, coupled with marketing and public awareness efforts both before Stagecoach took the franchise and with very astute management since, usage of the system has increased immensely over the past few years. Currently over 11.5 million passenger journeys are recorded each year. It will be of interest to readers to note that a staggering 47% increase was recorded between June 1996 and June 1997. The pattern of increasing patronage has been a continuing one since opening. At the same time bus patronage throughout the whole of South Yorkshire has dropped drastically. Currently the tram on its 29km of route, and operating within the City of Sheffield only, carries over 7% of the total public transport (including local rail) patronage for the County of South Yorkshire. There are 80,000 people living in a walking distance of the tramway.

South Yorkshire Passenger Transport Executive regularly measures reliability of transport operations and Supertram is consistently the leader. For example recently a very healthy 92% of all departures were recorded as on time. This is a fantastic tribute to the operation and its dedicated staff. Reliability of the vehicles is exceptional. Out of a fleet of 25 there is a current requirement for 22 vehicles in service, (23 in the morning peak). This is maintained virtually without exception. Since operation started in 1994 over 50 million passenger journeys have been made.

The tramway operates in a competitive environment, competing with other public transport operators. The potential for some form of integration is something the PTE is actively encouraging. Intermodal ticketing with the county's major bus company is in force but only in a minor way. Feeder bus services linking estates to the tramway are being looked at and recently the first Rural Bus scheme linking with the tramway has commenced operation.

In a recent study it was found that 22% of the current patronage previously used cars for the journey now undertaken by Supertram, either as driver or passenger. The same people were asked what they would do if the trams were taken off now. The same percentage indicated they would return to the car; they would not travel by bus – further proof of the ability of the tramway over its rubber tyred competitor. Light Rail is seen as convenient, comfortable, safe and secure with a high degree of service reliability and good accessibility.

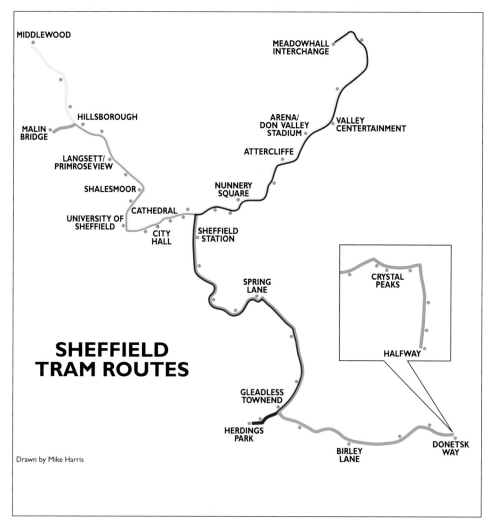

SHEFFIELD
TRAM ROUTES

Drawn by Mike Harris

THE SUPERTRAM VEHICLE

A full-scale mock up of the front portion was produced by Siemens/Duewag so that the people of Sheffield could see and comment on the future development.

A fleet of 25 double articulated, eight powered axle trams running on four bogies operates the tramway. Each vehicle is identical and measures 34.9 metres in length, 2.65 metres wide and weighing 52 tonnes unladen. These truly magnificent vehicles are some of the largest cars ever to be built for public transport and were constructed by the German manufacturer Siemens/Duewag at their Düsseldorf factory, sadly closed last year with manufacturing transferred to new premises. The design specification was very demanding – low floor entrances were essential to meet, as elsewhere, the requirements of a low platform system and to meet the needs of mobility impaired passengers, although the requirements of the Disability Discrimination Act were not in place when these cars were built in 1992–1994. The all-steel vehicles can comfortably accommodate 88 seated passengers, mainly in double facing seats with a standing capacity of 162 (4 per square metre). Two low-level areas by the doors in the end sections account for 40% of the total floor space and are laid out to provide accommodation for wheelchair users and/or mums and dads with babies in pushchairs.

Supertram is a bi-directional vehicle with an identical driving cab at each end, completely separate from the passenger area. The main service brake is a regenerative system (that is, the traction motors act as dynamos during braking and the recycled energy is returned to the power supply). There are also air-operated disc brakes on each axle and magnetic track brakes on each bogie. Intelligent computer terminals in the cabs and underfloor equipment compartments control heating, ventilation and safety systems feeding data to the vehicle's Central Control Unit. Constant monitoring equipment pinpoints and diagnoses any problem in the event of a fault and displays information for the driver on a panel in the cab. Drivers are in radio contact with the Central Control Room at all times. The first three trams were tested on the Rheinbahn system between Düsseldorf and nearby Krefeld.

View over the driver on tram test in Düsseldorf.

All the 25 vehicles were painted in what this author thought was a very attractive livery of Grey and Blue when they were delivered to Sheffield. A change early on in their careers brought a new logo to them encouraging passengers to 'Sit Back and Relax'. This of course brought comment when the trams were becoming full; one wit declared that passengers should 'Stand Up and Fume'. The system was reaching out to more and more customers!

On Stagecoach taking over the operation, the cars were painted in their house colours of white with Orange, Blue and Red hoops around the vehicle. Recently the skirts have been painted blue and the new Stagecoach logo has been added.

Vehicle 120 has been used as an all over advertising vehicle, firstly for a company who unfortunately went into liquidation, but now parades the streets in pink on one side and turquoise on the other advertising the Meadowhall Shopping Centre.

A tram in the latest livery has just left Sheffield Midland Station on a former road converted to tramway.

DEPOT

The original proposal was to have a depot situated in the south-east by Halfway terminus; however this was moved to Nunnery, at the request of SCC.

The Nunnery Depot is situated on the line to Meadowhall, and is the only depot on the current system. Its 2.6 hectare site consists of a workshop building, stabling for 24 trams, a stores building, engineering sidings, wheel lathe, vehicle washing equipment and sanding equipment – trams of course carry sand to assist in adhesion and braking. The first floor consists of the main operation and maintenance offices and staff facilities. In the south-east corner is located the Control Room. From here the operations and power controllers monitor the system around the clock using radio, AVL (Automatic Vehicle Location System) SCADA (Supervisory Control and Data Acquisition) and a link from Sheffield City Council's Urban Traffic Control traffic light operation. The SCADA system is used to control and monitor the Traction Power Supply. The master station equipment is located in the control room at the depot. It communicates with the Remote Terminal Units at each of the sub-stations. These provide facilities for the Power and Traffic Controllers to remotely operate the DC breakers for the OCS supply at any of the twelve sub-stations when necessary.

The depot is built on land which prior to Supertram had been used for railway activities.

PRIVATISATION OF THE OPERATION

South Yorkshire Supertram Ltd, the operating company (originally known as South Yorkshire Supertram (No. 2) Ltd,) holds the concession to operate and maintain the system until March 2024. It was this company which Stagecoach Holdings PLC acquired for £1.15 million on 17th December 1997. The company, whose trading name is Stagecoach Supertram, operates under a Concession Agreement with the PTE, and receives no operating subsidies. It is therefore responsible for its own operation and maintenance costs and of course revenue. A clause in the sale means that SYPTE will receive a small percentage of any profits made if the figure exceeds agreed levels during the first nine financial years.

The maintenance of the vehicles and infrastructure is in the hands of Porterbrook Maintenance Ltd under contract from Stagecoach Supertram.

South Yorkshire Light Rail Ltd (originally known as South Yorkshire Supertram Ltd) is the asset owner of the tramway. It was bought from the PTE by HSBC in 2000.

Prior to this sale certain assets had been sold in financial deals to banking interests. These assets consisted of the 25 trams, the wheel lathe and other items of equipment. The PTE still has responsibilities for the state, condition, change procedure and general asset management.

ADDITIONS TO THE SYSTEM

SYPTE has an important role in developing extensions, new interchanges and stops. Oscar Faber Consultants are currently employed studying the possibility of extending the tramway, not only within the City of Sheffield, but also throughout South Yorkshire. A new mini–interchange with links to the tramway at Hillsborough is currently under construction. A new stop has been provided for the redevelopment of Sheffield Station.